*If ever this vast country is brought under a single govern-
ment, it will be one of the most extensive corruptions.*
—Thomas Jefferson, 1822

Thomas Jefferson

"Enemy of Statism"

"Friend of Liberty"

*I would rather be exposed to the inconveniences attending
too much liberty, than those attending too small a degree of it.*
—Thomas Jefferson, 1791

*The God who gave us life, gave us liberty at the same time:
the hand of force may destroy, but cannot disjoin them.*
—Thomas Jefferson, 1808

About the Uncle Eric Series

The Uncle Eric series of books is written by Richard J. Maybury for young and old alike. Using the epistolary style of writing (using letters to tell a story), Mr. Maybury plays the part of an economist writing a series of letters to his niece or nephew. Using stories and examples, he gives interesting and clear explanations of topics that are generally thought to be too difficult for anyone but experts.

Mr. Maybury warns, "beware of anyone who tells you a topic is above you or better left to experts. Many people are twice as smart as they think they are, but they've been intimidated into believing some topics are above them. You can understand almost anything if it is explained well."

The series is called UNCLE ERIC'S MODEL OF HOW THE WORLD WORKS. In the series, Mr. Maybury writes from the political, legal, and economic viewpoint of America's Founders. The books can be read in any order and have been written to stand alone. To get the most from each one, however, Mr. Maybury suggests the following order of reading:

Uncle Eric's Model
of How the World Works

Uncle Eric Talks About Personal, Career, and Financial Security

Whatever Happened to Penny Candy?

Whatever Happened to Justice?

Are You Liberal? Conservative? or Confused?

Ancient Rome: How It Affects You Today

Evaluating Books: What Would Thomas Jefferson Think About This?

The Money Mystery

The Clipper Ship Strategy

The Thousand Year War in the Mideast

World War I: The Rest of the Story and How It Affects You Today

World War II: The Rest of the Story and How It Affects You Today

(Study guides available or forthcoming for above titles.)

An Uncle Eric Book

Evaluating Books

What Would Thomas Jefferson Think About This?

Guidelines for Selecting Books
Consistent with the
Principles of America's Founders

Second Edition

by Richard J. Maybury
(Uncle Eric)

published by
Bluestocking Press
www.BluestockingPress.com

Printed and bound in the United States of America.
Cover design by Brian C. Williams, El Dorado, CA
Edited by Jane A. Williams and Kathryn Daniels

Cover graphic used with permission: Copyrighted by the White House Historical Association; Photograph by the National Geographic Society. Thomas Jefferson, page 1, Painting by Rembrandt Peale. Courtesy Princeton University. Reproduced from the *Dictionary of American Portraits,* published by Dover Publications, Inc., 1967. Thomas Jefferson, profile graphic which faces quotes throughout book: Painting attributed to James Sharples, Sr. Courtesy Independence National Historical Park. Reproduced from the *Dictionary of American Portraits,* published by Dover Publications, Inc., 1967.

Library of Congress Cataloging-in-Publication Data

Maybury, Rick.
    Evaluating books : what would Thomas Jefferson think about this? : guidelines for selecting books consistent with the principles of America's founders / by Richard J. Maybury (Uncle Eric) .-- 2nd ed.
        p. cm. -- (An "Uncle eric" book)
    Includes bibliographical references and index.
    ISBN-13: 978-0-942617-53-5
    ISBN-10: 0-942617-53-3 (soft cover : alk. paper)
    1. Books and reading--United States. 2. Libertarianism--United States. I. Title.

Z1003.2.M38 2004
028'.9--dc22   2004007439

Published by Bluestocking Press • P.O. Box 1014
Placerville, CA 95667-1014
web site: www.BluestockingPress.com

To M,
my closest friend and one of the finest people
I've ever known. She taught me compassion,
and changed me in a hundred ways. I miss her.

> ...the entire [Uncle Eric] series should be a required, integral, component of the social studies curriculum in all public and private schools. This would bring a quantum leap upward in the quality of citizenship in this country in a single generation.
> —William P. Snavely
> Emeritus Professor of Economics
> George Mason University

Uncle Eric's Model
of How the World Works

What is a model? In his book UNCLE ERIC TALKS ABOUT PERSONAL, CAREER, AND FINANCIAL SECURITY, Richard Maybury (Uncle Eric) explains that one of the most important things you can teach children or learn yourself is:

> Models are how we think, they are how we understand how the world works. As we go through life we build these very complex pictures in our minds of how the world works, and we're constantly referring back to them—matching incoming data against our models. That's how we make sense of things.
>
> One of the most important uses for models is in sorting incoming information to decide if it's important or not.
>
> In most schools, models are never mentioned because the teachers are unaware of them. One of the most dangerous weaknesses in traditional education is that it contains no model for political history. Teachers teach what they were taught—and no one ever mentioned models to them, so they don't teach them to their students.

For the most part, children are just loaded down with collections of facts that they are made to memorize. Without good models, children have no way to know which facts are important and which are not. Students leave school thinking history is a senseless waste of time. Then, deprived of the real lessons of history, the student is vulnerable.

The question is, which models to teach. Mr. Maybury says, "The two models that I think are crucially important for everyone to learn are economics and law."

WHATEVER HAPPENED TO PENNY CANDY? explains the economic model, which is based on Austrian economics, the most free-market of all economic models. WHATEVER HAPPENED TO JUSTICE? explains the legal model and shows the connection between rational law and economic progress. The legal model is the old British common law—or Natural Law. The original principles on which America was founded were those of the old British common law.

These two books, PENNY CANDY and JUSTICE, provide the overall model of how human civilization works, especially the world of money.

Once the model is understood, read ARE YOU LIBERAL? CONSERVATIVE? OR CONFUSED? This book explains political philosophies relative to Uncle Eric's Model—and makes a strong case for consistency to that model, no exceptions.

Next, read ANCIENT ROME: HOW IT AFFECTS YOU TODAY, which shows what happens when a society ignores Uncle Eric's Model and embraces fascism—an all too common practice these days, although the word fascism is never used.

To help you locate books and authors generally in agreement with these economic and legal models, Mr. Maybury wrote EVALUATING BOOKS: WHAT WOULD THOMAS JEFFERSON THINK ABOUT THIS? This book provides guidelines for selecting books that are consistent with the principles of America's Founders. You can apply these guidelines to books, movies, news commentators, and current events—to any spoken or written medium.

Further expanding on the economic model, THE MONEY MYSTERY explains the hidden force affecting your career, business, and investments. Some economists refer to this force as velocity, others to money demand. Whichever term is used, it is one of the least understood forces affecting your life. Knowing about velocity and money demand not only gives you an understanding of history that few others have, it prepares you to understand and avoid pitfalls in your career, business, and investments. THE MONEY MYSTERY is the first sequel to WHATEVER HAPPENED TO PENNY CANDY? It provides essential background for getting the most from THE CLIPPER SHIP STRATEGY.

THE CLIPPER SHIP STRATEGY explains how government's interference in the economy affects business, careers, and investments. It's a practical nuts-and-bolts strategy for prospering in our turbulent economy. This book is the second sequel to WHATEVER HAPPENED TO PENNY CANDY? and should be read after THE MONEY MYSTERY.

THE THOUSAND YEAR WAR IN THE MIDEAST: HOW IT AFFECTS YOU TODAY explains how events on the other side of the world a thousand years ago can affect us more than events in our own hometowns today. In the last quarter of the 20th century, the Thousand Year War has been the cause of great shocks to the investment markets—the oil embargoes, the Iranian hostage crisis, the Iraq-Kuwait war, the Caucasus Wars over the Caspian Sea oil basin, and September 11, 2001—and it is likely to remain so for decades to come. Forewarned is forearmed. You must understand where this war is leading to manage your career, business, and investments.

The explosion of the battleship Maine in Havana Harbor in 1898 was the beginning of a chain reaction that eventually led to the destruction of the World Trade Center. In his two-part World War series Richard Maybury explains that an unbroken line leads directly from the Spanish-American War through World War I, World War II, the Korean and Vietnam Wars, the Iraq-Kuwait War, and the "War on Terror" that began September 11, 2001. Mr. Maybury explains the other side of the story, the side you are not likely to get anywhere else, in this two-part World War series: WORLD WAR I: THE REST OF THE STORY AND HOW IT AFFECTS YOU TODAY and WORLD WAR II: THE REST OF THE STORY AND HOW IT AFFECTS YOU TODAY.

Uncle Eric's Model
of How the World Works

These books can be read in any order and have been written to stand alone. But to get the most from each one, Mr. Maybury suggests the following order of reading:

Book 1.   UNCLE ERIC TALKS ABOUT PERSONAL, CAREER, AND FINANCIAL SECURITY.
Uncle Eric's Model introduced. Models (or paradigms) are how people think; they are how we understand our world. To achieve success in our careers, investments, and every other part of our lives, we need sound models. These help us recognize and use the information that is important and bypass that which is not. In this book, Mr. Maybury introduces the model he has found most useful. These are explained in WHATEVER HAPPENED TO PENNY CANDY? WHATEVER HAPPENED TO JUSTICE? and THE CLIPPER SHIP STRATEGY.
(Study Guide available.)

Book 2. WHATEVER HAPPENED TO PENNY CANDY? A FAST, CLEAR, AND FUN EXPLANATION OF THE ECONOMICS YOU NEED FOR SUCCESS IN YOUR CAREER, BUSINESS, AND INVESTMENTS.
The economic model explained. The clearest and most interesting explanation of economics around. Learn about investment cycles, velocity, business cycles, recessions, inflation, money demand, and more. Contains "Beyond the Basics," which supplements the basic ideas and is included for readers who choose to tackle more challenging concepts. Recommended by former U.S. Treasury Secretary William Simon and many others. *(Study Guide available.)*

Book 3. WHATEVER HAPPENED TO JUSTICE?
The legal model explained. Explores America's legal heritage. Shows what is wrong with our legal system and economy, and how to fix it. Discusses the difference between Higher Law and man-made law, and the connection between rational law and economic prosperity. Introduces the Two Laws: 1) Do all you have agreed to do. 2) Do not encroach on other persons or their property.
(Study Guide available.)

Book 4. ARE YOU LIBERAL? CONSERVATIVE? OR CONFUSED?
Political labels. What do they mean? Liberal, conservative, left, right, democrat, republican, moderate, socialist, libertarian, communist—what are their economic policies, and what plans do their promoters have for your money? Clear, concise explanations. Facts and fallacies.
(Study Guide available.)

Book 5.   ANCIENT ROME: HOW IT AFFECTS YOU TODAY.
This book explains what happens when a society
ignores the model. Are we heading for fascism
like ancient Rome? Mr. Maybury uses historical
events to explain current events, including the wars
in the former Soviet Empire, and the legal and
economic problems of America today. With the
turmoil in Russia and Russia's return to fascism,
you must read this book to understand your future. History does repeat.
(Study Guide available.)

Book 6.   EVALUATING BOOKS: WHAT WOULD THOMAS JEFFERSON
THINK ABOUT THIS?
Most books, magazines, and news stories are
slanted against the principles of America's
Founders. Often the writers are not aware of it,
they simply write as they were taught. Learn how
to identify the bias so you can make informed reading, listening, and viewing choices.

Book 7.   THE MONEY MYSTERY: THE HIDDEN FORCE AFFECTING
YOUR CAREER, BUSINESS, AND INVESTMENTS.
The first sequel to WHATEVER HAPPENED TO PENNY
CANDY? Some economists refer to velocity, others
to money demand. However it is seen, it is one of
the least understood forces affecting our businesses, careers, and investments—it is the financial trigger. This book discusses precautions you
should take and explains why Federal Reserve
officials remain so afraid of inflation. THE MONEY
MYSTERY prepares you to understand and avoid
pitfalls in your career, business, and investments.
(Study Guide available.)

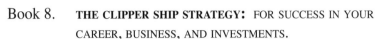

Book 8.   **THE CLIPPER SHIP STRATEGY:** FOR SUCCESS IN YOUR CAREER, BUSINESS, AND INVESTMENTS.
The second sequel to WHATEVER HAPPENED TO PENNY CANDY? Conventional wisdom says that when the government expands the money supply, the money descends on the economy in a uniform blanket. This is wrong. The money is injected into specific locations causing hot spots or "cones" such as the tech bubble of the 1990s. Mr. Maybury explains his system for tracking and profiting from these cones. Practical nuts-and-bolts strategy for prospering in our turbulent economy.
(Study Guide available.)

Book 9.   **THE THOUSAND YEAR WAR IN THE MIDEAST:** HOW IT AFFECTS YOU TODAY.
Mr. Maybury shows that events on the other side of the world a thousand years ago can affect us more than events in our hometowns today. This book explains the ten-century battle the U.S. has entered against the Islamic world. It predicted the events that began unfolding on September 11, 2001. It helps you understand the thinking of the Muslims in the Mideast, and why the coming oil war will affect investment markets around the globe. In the last three decades this war has been the cause of great shocks to the economy and investment markets, including the oil embargoes, the Iranian hostage crisis, the Iraq-Kuwait war, the Caucasus Wars over the Caspian Sea oil basin, and the September 11th attack—and it is likely to remain so for decades to come. Forewarned is forearmed. To successfully manage your career,

business, and investments, you must understand this war. *(Contact Bluestocking Press regarding Study Guide availability.)*

Book 10. **WORLD WAR I:** THE REST OF THE STORY AND HOW IT AFFECTS YOU TODAY, 1870 TO 1935.

The explosion of the battleship Maine in Havana Harbor in 1898 was the beginning of a chain reaction that continues today. Mr. Maybury presents an idea-based explanation of the First World War. He focuses on the ideas and events that led to World War I, events during the war, and how they led to World War II. Includes the ten deadly ideas that lead to war. *(Contact Bluestocking Press regarding Study Guide availability.)*

Book 11. **WORLD WAR II:** THE REST OF THE STORY AND HOW IT AFFECTS YOU TODAY, 1935 TO SEPTEMBER 11, 2001.

An idea-based explanation of the war. Focuses on events in the Second World War and how our misunderstanding of this war led to America's subsequent wars, including the Korean and Vietnam Wars, the Iraq-Kuwait War, and the "War on Terror" that began September 11, 2001. *(Contact Bluestocking Press regarding Study Guide availability.)*

Quantity Discounts
Available

The Uncle Eric books are available at special quantity discounts for bulk purchases to individuals, businesses, schools, libraries, and associations.

For terms and discount schedule contact:

Special Sales Department
Bluestocking Press
Phone: 800-959-8586
email: CustomerService@BluestockingPress.com
web site: www.BluestockingPress.com

Specify how books are to be distributed: for classrooms, or as gifts, premiums, fund raisers — or to be resold.

Study Guides Available

for Richard J. Maybury's Uncle Eric books

BLUESTOCKING GUIDES

by Jane A. Williams and / or Kathryn Daniels

BLUESTOCKING GUIDES are designed to enhance a student's understanding and retention of the subject matter presented in the corresponding primers.

BLUESTOCKING GUIDES include some or all of the following: comprehension questions and answers (relating to specific chapters within the primer), thought questions to facilitate student-instructor discussion, application questions (to guide the student in applying the concepts learned to everyday life), research and essay assignments, suggestions for further reading and/ or viewing, and a final exam.

Order from your favorite book store or direct from the publisher: Bluestocking Press (see order information on last page of this book).

Contents

Author's Disclosure

For reasons I do not understand, writers today are supposed to be objective. Few disclose the viewpoints or opinions they use to decide what information is important and what is not, or what shall be presented or omitted.

I do not adhere to this standard and make no pretense of being objective. I am biased in favor of liberty, free markets, and international neutrality and proud of it. So I disclose my viewpoint, which you will find explained in detail in my other books.[1]

For those who have not yet read these publications, I call my viewpoint Juris Naturalism (pronounced *jur*-es *nach*-e-re-liz-em, sometimes abbreviated JN) meaning the belief in a natural law that is higher than any government's law. Here are six quotes from America's Founders that help to describe this viewpoint:

> ...all men are created equal, that they are endowed by their Creator with certain unalienable rights.
> —Declaration of Independence, 1776

> The natural rights of the colonists are these: first, a right to life; second to liberty; third to property; together with the right to support and defend them in the best manner they can.
> —Samuel Adams, 1772

---

[1] See Richard Maybury's other Uncle Eric books (see pgs. 6-13), published by Bluestocking Press, phone: 800-959-8586, web site: www.BluestockingPress.com

It is strangely absurd to suppose that a million of human beings collected together are not under the same moral laws which bind each of them separately.
—Thomas Jefferson, 1816

A wise and frugal government, which shall restrain men from injuring one another, which shall leave them otherwise free to regulate their own pursuits of industry and improvement, and shall not take from the mouth of labor the bread it has earned. This is the sum of good government.
—Thomas Jefferson, 1801

Not a place on earth might be so happy as America. Her situation is remote from all the wrangling world, and she has nothing to do but to trade with them.
—Thomas Paine, 1776

The great rule of conduct for us, in regard to foreign nations, is, in extending our commercial relations, to have with them as little political connection as possible.
—George Washington, 1796

George
Washington

How to Use This Book

The Uncle Eric books are a series. Each book builds on those that precede it. Although each book can stand alone, it will be clearer and more helpful if you first read the following two books that explain Uncle Eric's Model, which is a two-part model based on free market economics and Higher Law principles: 1. WHATEVER HAPPENED TO PENNY CANDY? and 2. WHATEVER HAPPENED TO JUSTICE?

WHATEVER HAPPENED TO PENNY CANDY? explains economics. WHATEVER HAPPENED TO JUSTICE? explains law and the connection between law and economics. (Student study guides are available that complement most of the Uncle Eric books.)

A good way to use EVALUATING BOOKS: WHAT WOULD THOMAS JEFFERSON THINK ABOUT THIS? is to read it twice. First go through it cover to cover underlining points most important to you. Also make a list of the recommended books and other publications you'll want to read. After you've read these, reread EVALUATING BOOKS: WHAT WOULD THOMAS JEFFERSON THINK ABOUT THIS? and refer back to the others wherever appropriate. This will give you the foundation you need to confidently select books consistent with the principles on which America was founded.

**What Would
Thomas Jefferson
Think About This?**

Only lay down true principles, and adhere to them inflexibly.

—Thomas Jefferson, 1816

Evaluating Books

Dear Reader,

My purpose here is to help you avoid books that teach misleading or harmful information, especially information that is contrary to basic American principles described in the writings of Thomas Jefferson and the other American Founders.

My focus is on **political power**[2]. As explained in WHAT-EVER HAPPENED TO JUSTICE?[3] political power is the privilege of using force on persons who have not harmed anyone. This is what sets government apart from businesses, churches, charities, and other private organizations. No private organization can legally send men with guns to your home to force you to obey its wishes.

It will be of little avail to the people that the laws are made by men of their own choice if the laws be so voluminous that they cannot be read, or so incoherent that they cannot be understood.

—James Madison, 1787

The coercive nature of political power is why America's Founders believed this power is inherently evil, it corrupts. They

---

[2] Political power: the legalized privilege of initiating the use of force on persons who have not harmed anyone. This privilege distinguishes government from all other institutions.

[3] WHATEVER HAPPENED TO JUSTICE? by Richard J. Maybury, an Uncle Eric book, published by Bluestocking Press, phone: 800-959-8586, web site: www.BluestockingPress.com

were trying to set up a government that would have extremely limited power so that it would not be able to do much damage.

The Founders were convinced that governments are, fundamentally, predators. These predators must be kept small and weak or they will destroy law and devour the country.[4]

What Would Thomas Jefferson Think About This?

I think we have more machinery of government than is necessary, too many parasites living on the labor of the industries.
—Thomas Jefferson, 1824

Jefferson wrote these words when the Federal government had only about 8,500 civilian employees; today it has about three million.

The prevailing political viewpoints today[5] are the opposite of the original American philosophy. They contend that

---

[4] For those who believe it can't happen in America, read MANZANAR by John Armor and Peter Wright, published by Vintage, a division of Random House. Also read Roy Uyeda's real-life story, available from Bluestocking Press, web site: www.BluestockingPress.com, phone: 800-959-8586. Both are about the Japanese internment that took place in America during World War II.

[5] For more about political viewpoints, read ARE YOU LIBERAL? CONSERVATIVE? OR CONFUSED? by Richard J. Maybury, an Uncle Eric book, published by Bluestocking Press, phone: 800-959-8586, web site: www.BluestockingPress.com.

government is our friend, our protector, the solution to our problems, and that political power is wonderful stuff and everyone should have some of it.

These prevailing philosophies can be grouped under the label **statism**. **Statists**[6] advocate the use of political power to achieve whatever they think necessary.

Many statists believe political power is a fine and necessary tool for reorganizing the economy, meaning for reorganizing your work, production, and trade—they wish to control you by force.

Schoolbooks are saturated with statism. This is not to say textbook writers have formed a conspiracy to brainwash students. In most cases the writers do not know they are teaching concepts that are the opposite of the original American philosophy. They teach only what they were taught.

Rarely will you find a book that adheres 100% to the original American philosophy, which I introduced in WHAT-EVER HAPPENED TO JUSTICE? Students *will be* exposed to statism. You will need to decide how much exposure you want them to have. The more they know about the original American philosophy and economics, the more statism they can read without being seriously misled.

A good way to judge how ready students are is to ask them to argue both sides of a variety of issues. From newspapers, "reputable"[7] on-line media reports, or TV, select stories that raise questions about law, government, economics, or foreign

---

[6] Statist: One who advocates a large, powerful government.

[7] Reputable on-line media. Means recognized authorities such as: government sources, recognized experts in their fields, university or college research studies, etc.

policy. Have someone take the pro-liberty side and the student take the statist side. Midway through the debate, at a time of your choosing, suddenly switch sides. Then switch back, and back again.

The student should be persuasive on either side. This indicates deep knowledge about the subject.

Books that will help you with this are the "Opposing Viewpoints" series published by Greenhaven Press (www.gale.com) and the "Evaluating Viewpoints: Critical Thinking in United States History" series published by The Critical Thinking Co. (www.criticalthinking.com). Also, visit World Press Review's web site (www.worldpress.org).

Don't use any product blindly. Use the source documents to help with your debates, but be alert to any accompanying editorializing.

But, you ask, if the student knows that much about statism, doesn't this run the risk that the student will be seduced by the statist side?

No. You know your student. Is the student dedicated to Higher Law, meaning the two fundamental laws explained in WHATEVER HAPPENED TO JUSTICE?[8] If yes, you have nothing to worry about. If the student is dedicated to Higher Law and can argue both sides of a variety of issues, then the student can be safely exposed to any statist literature. For sources of books and other materials that adhere closely to American principles see the "Recommended Reading and Listening" sections of this book.

---

[8] For a further explanation of the two fundamental laws, refer to the example articles in this book: *A Tribute to the Statue of Ellis Island* and *The Founding Fathers: Smugglers, Tax Evaders, and Traitors?*, as well as the book WHATEVER HAPPENED TO JUSTICE? by Richard J. Maybury, an Uncle Eric book, published by Bluestocking Press, phone: 800-959-8586, web site: www.BluestockingPress.com

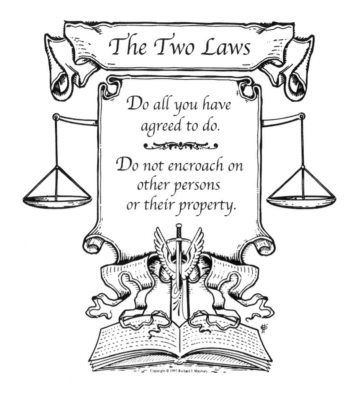

The Two Laws

Do all you have agreed to do.

Do not encroach on other persons or their property.

Copyright © 1993 Richard J. Maybury

To judge a book I suggest you use a point system. Add points for each mention of the costs or dangers of political power and subtract points for anything that legitimizes political power. The higher the score the better the book.

Bear in mind that statist viewpoints are seldom voiced outright. Often they are presented subtly; readers are led to jump to conclusions that are not true.

Also remember that our reading of history forms our attitudes. We make decisions on the basis of what we believe worked or didn't work in the past. So, he who controls the slant of the history books controls our thoughts and therefore our actions. This is the most important reason for parents and guardians to screen the books their children read. To fail to screen is to leave the child's mind, and his future, in the hands of persons who have never met him and may care nothing about him. Some persons may even have a hidden agenda that includes using the student as an expendable pawn.

What Would Thomas Jefferson Think About This?

Reading, reflection and time have convinced me that the interests of society require the observation of those moral precepts only in which all religions agree (for all forbid us to murder, steal, plunder, or bear false witness) ... The varieties in structure and action of the human mind as in those of the body, are the work of our Creator, against which it cannot be a religious duty to erect the standard of uniformity.
—Thomas Jefferson, 1809

The books and audio material that are listed in the "Recommended Reading and Listening" sections throughout this book have been selected because they tend to be politically consistent with original American principles, but this is not meant to be a blanket endorsement of these resources. Parental discretion is always advised.

For an excellent—and frightening—example of what *not* to teach students, read the two highly acclaimed books by historian Howard Zinn, A PEOPLE'S HISTORY OF THE UNITED STATES and DECLARATIONS OF INDEPENDENCE (both published by HarperCollins). These are cleverly disguised statism. They attempt to discredit virtually everything America stood for originally. Expose your student to them only *after* the student has a good background in free market economics, common law, and the beliefs of America's Founders. Such books receive rave reviews because few reviewers have this background.

Author Zinn advocates overthrow of the existing order in America—which by itself is not necessarily a bad idea—but what do we replace it with? Zinn ridicules common law and free markets, so the system of liberty is out according to him.

He does give a vague description of a new order of "cooperation" but his plan is so lacking in specifics that it would surely lead to chaos. We can look to Yugoslavia in 1991 as an example of what can happen. The existing order was overthrown without anyone having a clear notion of a workable alternative. Several wars broke out and, by the end of the decade, hundreds of thousands had been killed.

The same thing happened in Iraq in 2004. Saddam Hussein's regime had been eliminated in 2003, but the Iraqi people had no experience and little knowledge of other ways to organize things—so they began fighting among themselves.

At bottom, there are only three possible political conditions: liberty, tyranny, or chaos. In Asia, Africa, and other parts of the world where few people have much experience or knowledge of liberty, there are only two possible conditions: tyranny and chaos. If we remove tyranny, there is only one possibility: chaos.

Until the collapse of the Soviet Union, most statists advocated overthrow of the existing order in the United States and replacement with **socialism**[9]. But the clear failure of the socialist economies now leaves statists with no new plan. Zinn's suggestion, which is representative of those popular now, seems to be a kind of utopia. He writes,

> Everyone could share the routine but necessary jobs for a few hours a day, and leave most of the time free for enjoyment, creativity, labors of love, and yet produce enough for an equal and ample distribution of goods. Certain basic things would be abundant enough to be taken out of the money system and be available—free—to everyone: food, housing, health care, education, transportation.

No kidding, that's what this eminent historian promises, free lunches.

Statist books usually do expose many hidden and unpleasant truths about America, which is why they can be so persuasive to young minds that have been fed only whitewash all their lives. Zinn's work is an excellent example of such criticisms. It drags many skeletons out of the American closet, which is good, but these skeletons really amount to no more than proof that America's Founders didn't get it all perfect on the first try. Someone who comes to these statist works unprepared can be terribly shaken by them.

---

[9] Socialism: an economic system in which (1) the government has monopoly control and ownership of all means of production, (2) the government is in the hands of socialists, and (3) there is only one employer, the government.

Statist books should be an integral part of your student's learning *after* the student is thoroughly grounded in the legal and economic principles on which America was founded.

You won't have any trouble finding statist works. Use the history, economics, and political science books on the approved textbook lists for almost any public school system.

Beginning on page 35 of this book are some "Negative Indicators"—statist viewpoints and half-truths—to watch for. On pages 77-81 are Misleading Terms. Positive Indicators are listed on pages 83-103. But first, I'll answer a question you might be asking: "Just who were America's Founders, and why the emphasis on Thomas Jefferson?"

—Richard J. Maybury
(Uncle Eric)

America's Founders

The American Revolution was in two parts. The first was the war surrounding the 1776 Declaration of Independence. The second was the creation of the 1787 Constitution and 1791 Bill of Rights.

Any prominent person who was influential in either of these parts and who was in general or exact agreement with the principles described in my book WHATEVER HAPPENED TO JUSTICE? should be called an American Founder. I could list hundreds, but the twelve Founders listed on the following pages are the most well known.

Thomas Jefferson and Thomas Paine were probably the most important—they gave guidance by articulating the principles. Not that others didn't give guidance, but Jefferson and Paine gave the most.

Unfortunately, this guidance has been almost entirely erased from American culture and American history. Few Americans today know anything about the principles of the Founders; history has become little more than a list of names, dates, and wars. I urge you to read the works of the Founders; you will find them most enlightening.

In a recent survey, new college graduates listed history as the academic subject whose lessons they found of least use in their daily lives.

—William Straus & Neil Howe
GENERATIONS, 1991

- John Adams. A key leader of the attempt to overthrow the existing government and to establish a new one, Adams also traveled to Europe as a diplomat. There he observed that people who had little understanding of liberty could not maintain a free society. He was appalled but not surprised when the French Revolution, which was an attempt to copy the American Revolution, led to the Reign of Terror because the French did not have the background in the principles of liberty that Americans did.

- Samuel Adams. A leader of the Boston Tea Party, Sam Adams was one of the most radical of the American rebels and one of the most influential in persuading the colonists to overthrow their government. Lt. Gov. Thomas Hutchinson complained that Adams was the greatest "incendiary" in the British Empire.

- Benjamin Franklin. A printer, essayist, scientist, rebel leader, inventor, diplomat, and philosopher, Franklin was as respected in Europe as in America. He was the first American to be a key figure in world history. His credibility led many European leaders to take the American Revolution seriously and to give America a fair hearing. By this means, Franklin helped open a gateway for American principles to spread around the world.

- Alexander Hamilton. Before his 30th birthday, Hamilton had been a distinguished military officer, knew intimately most of the leaders of the American Revolution, and was recognized as one of the best lawyers in America. In debates over the Constitution, he argued that democracy is an enemy of liberty—it is little more than mob rule—and a new layer of government was needed to keep the state democracies from running wild. In Federalist Paper #15, for instance, he wrote, "Has it been found that bodies of men act with more rectitude or greater disinterestedness than individuals? The contrary of this has been inferred by all accurate observers of the conduct of mankind; and the inference is founded upon obvious reasons. Regard to reputation has a less active influence when the infamy of a bad action is to be divided among a number than when it is to fall singly upon one."

• John Hancock. A prominent leader of the rebellion and first signer of the Declaration of Independence, Hancock was known as "the Prince of Smugglers"—he was earning his living by evading the government's trade restrictions and taxes long before the rebellion began.

• Patrick Henry. The leading orator of the rebellion, Patrick Henry became famous by opposing the government's Stamp Act with the announcement, "Caesar had his Brutus, Charles I his Cromwell, and George III—may he profit from their example." This was a thinly veiled threat suggesting the king should be assassinated. After the revolution, as leader of the anti-Federalists, Henry opposed creation of the U.S. Government, warning that it would eventually grow so powerful, meddlesome, and tax-hungry it would destroy our liberty.

• John Jay. At first, Jay opposed overthrowing the British government but, after the Declaration of Independence, he worked hard to insure the success of the revolution. An author of the Federalist Papers, he argued for creation of the Federal government and became the first Chief Justice of the Supreme Court.

- Thomas Jefferson. Architect, scientist, farmer, and primary author of the Declaration of Independence, Jefferson was the leading philosopher of the revolution. The clarity of his prolific writings offer the most complete explanations of American principles.

- James Madison. A leader of the revolution, Madison was also the most influential light behind the Constitution and he sponsored the Bill of Rights. His chief argument for creation of the Federal government was that this new layer of government was necessary to limit democracy in order to protect liberty.

- George Mason. Principle architect of the Virginia Declaration of Rights, which became the model for the U.S. Bill of Rights, Mason was a leader of the anti-Federalists and voted against creation of the Federal government.

- Thomas Paine. It would be hard to imagine an independent America without Thomas Paine. His pamphlet COMMON SENSE rallied the people behind the Declaration of Independence, and his series of pamphlets called The Crisis continued to generate support and boost morale. He wanted to sign on as a soldier but George Washington would not let him, explaining that Paine's writings were too important for his talents to be risked on the battlefield.

- George Washington. Commanding general of the rebel army, Washington is one of history's most outstanding examples of persons dedicated to the belief that there is a Higher Law than any human law. In 1782-83, army officers in Newburgh, New York were angry at Congress's failure to pay their wages. They proposed to establish a military dictatorship and make Washington king of America. He declined and instead argued that soldiers should refuse to obey the orders of an officer who attempts "to overturn the liberties of our country," and advised them to "express your utmost horror and detestation" of such an officer.

Recommended Listening

- COMMON SENSE, THOMAS PAINE; THE DECLARATION OF INDEPENDENCE, THOMAS JEFFERSON

- THE WEALTH OF NATIONS, ADAM SMITH

- THE FEDERALIST PAPERS, ALEXANDER HAMILTON, JAMES MADISON, JOHN JAY

- TWO TREATISES ON GOVERNMENT, JOHN LOCKE

- DEMOCRACY IN AMERICA, ALEXIS DE TOCQUEVILLE

- THE CONSTITUTIONAL CONVENTION

- THE RATIFICATION DEBATES

- THE TEXT OF THE U.S. CONSTITUTION

- THE BILL OF RIGHTS AND ADDITIONAL AMENDMENTS.

The above audio presentations are produced by Knowledge Products, Nashville, TN. For ages 14 up.

Negative Indicators

The General Statist Viewpoint

The general statist viewpoint is that political power is good and everyone should have lots of it. Its benefits are greater than its costs, and it can solve our problems.

This is the unspoken statist viewpoint found in virtually all school books published today.

The Other Side of the Story

The "other side of the story" says that a book can be factual without being truthful. A clever writer can make any viewpoint sound plausible simply by presenting facts that support the viewpoint and omitting facts that refute it. His presentation will be factual but misleading.[10]

What I attempt to do in my books is present the omitted facts—the other side of the story—the way I believe America's Founders would want these facts presented. The Founders hated political power, were afraid of it, and believed it was fundamentally evil. They believed the only "real world" solution was to keep power widely dispersed and so limited that no one had much interest in it—it was virtually irrelevant.

---

[10] Three books written to give multiple viewpoints are: BULL RUN by Paul Fleischman, published by Harper Collins, NY. INDIAN, SOLDIER, AND SETTLER, by Robert M. Utley, published by Jefferson National Expansion Historical Association, Inc., St. Louis, MO, and THROUGH INDIAN EYES: THE NATIVE EXPERIENCE IN BOOKS FOR CHILDREN, edited by Beverly Slapin and Doris Seale, published by UCLA American Indian Studies Center, Los Angeles, CA.

What Would Thomas Jefferson Think About This?

...a wise and frugal government, which shall restrain men from injuring one another, which shall leave them otherwise free to regulate their own pursuits of industry and improvement, and shall not take from the mouth of labor the bread it has earned. This is the sum of good government.

—Thomas Jefferson, 1801

Sometimes it is said that man cannot be trusted with the government of himself. Can he, then, be trusted with the government of others?

—Thomas Jefferson, 1801

The following pages include specific issues giving the statist viewpoint and "other side of the story."

Issue #1

The Great Depression

Statist Viewpoint

The Great Depression[11] was caused by a failure of capitalism[12] or free enterprise.

The Other Side of the Story

The Great Depression was caused by the Federal Reserve. In the 1920s, officials inflated the currency and thereby caused massive amounts of malinvestment.

Malinvestment is mistaken investment. Investment is the production of factories, office buildings, machinery, and other *tools* necessary to create jobs.

> *...All the perplexities, confusion and distress in America arise, not from the defects in their constitution or confederation, not from want of honor or virtue, so much as from downright ignorance of the nature of coin, credit and circulation...*
>
> —John Quincy Adams, 1829

---

[11] Great Depression. The wave of business failures, bankruptcies, unemployment, and poverty that struck much of the world during the 1930s.

[12] Capitalism. An economic system characterized by the private ownership of property, free trade, free speech and press, and minimal taxes and regulations.

Malinvestment is the formation of these tools in locations or ways that are not viable when the money supply stops expanding.

In other words, when the Federal Reserve injects money into the economy, this money distorts prices and profits. Firms and individuals are lured into making mistakes — malinvestments — that must be corrected. The correction period is a depression.

The 1920s inflation of the money supply led to the 1930s Great Depression which was the worst in U.S. history.

**What Would
Thomas Jefferson
Think About This?**

That paper money has some advantages, is admitted. But that its abuses also are inevitable, and, by breaking up the measure of value, makes a lottery of all private property, cannot be denied. Shall we ever be able to put a constitutional veto on it?

—Thomas Jefferson, 1817

Recommended Reading

- AMERICA'S GREAT DEPRESSION, 5ᵗʰ ed. by Murray Rothbard. Available from Laissez Faire Books, phone: 800-326-0996, web site: http://LFB.com. For ages 15 and up.

- WHAT YOU SHOULD KNOW ABOUT INFLATION by Henry Hazlitt. Published by Funk & Wagnalls, NY, 1968. For ages 14 and up.

- WHATEVER HAPPENED TO PENNY CANDY? by Richard J. Maybury, an Uncle Eric book. Published by Bluestocking Press, phone: 800-959-8586, web site: www.BluestockingPress.com. For ages 10 and up.

- THE CLIPPER SHIP STRATEGY by Richard J. Maybury, an Uncle Eric book. Published by Bluestocking Press, web site: www.BluestockingPress.com, phone: 800-959-8586. For ages 14 and up.

Issue #2

Franklin Roosevelt's New Deal

Statist Viewpoint

Franklin Roosevelt's New Deal[13] ended the Great Depression.

The Other Side of the Story

The Japanese navy ended the Great Depression. The New Deal probably prolonged the depression by delaying correction of the malinvestments.

The government's own statistics on unemployment and production show clearly that the depression was still on in 1939, six years after the New Deal began.

When Pearl Harbor was bombed, the government had an excuse to inflate with wild abandon to pay for the war. This flood of money breathed new life into the malinvestment, much of which is still with us today.

Incidentally, some scholars say that World War II prolonged the depression. In common usage, the word depression means a decline in gross domestic product and a rise in unemployment. Under this usage, the war ended the depression. However, I believe that the quality of life of John Q.

---

[13] New Deal. The term for the dollar devaluation, inflation of the money supply, trade restrictions, welfare programs, and other economic measures enacted during the Great Depression of the 1930s.

American is what really matters. Since John Q. American's standard of living did not increase during the war, one might be justified in saying the Great Depression did not end until the late 1940s.

Also, nothing I've written here or anywhere else should be taken to mean I agree with the old saying that war is good for the economy. This saying is widely believed, and I can think of nothing more evil. The economy is not a machine, it is people; killing people is not good for them.

Recommended Reading

- WORLD WAR II: THE REST OF THE STORY AND HOW IT AFFECTS YOU TODAY, an Uncle Eric book, by Richard J. Maybury. Part two of a two-part series on the world wars. Published by Bluestocking Press, web site: www.BluestockingPress.com, phone: 800-959-8586.

- HISTORICAL STATISTICS OF THE UNITED STATES, Bureau of the Census, Government Printing Office. See the unemployment, per capita, GNP, and money supply statistics relating to the 1920s and 1930s.

Issue #3

Progressive Taxes

Statist Viewpoint

Progressive taxes are good. (Under a "progressive" tax, persons who earn more pay more.)

The Other Side of the Story

If "progressive" pricing of government services is good, why not progressive pricing of everything? If you earn twice as much as your neighbor, you pay twice as much for bread, shoes, housing, etc. Think about it.

Recommended Reading

- ECONOMICS IN ONE LESSON (See Chapter 5) by Henry Hazlitt, Crown. Published by Crown, New York. For ages 14 and up.

What Would
Thomas Jefferson
Think About This?

If we run into such [government] debts, as that we must be taxed in our meat and in our drink, in our necessaries and our comforts, in our labors and our amusements, for our callings and our creeds, as the people of England are, our people, like them, must come to labor sixteen hours in the twenty-four, give the earnings of fifteen of these to the government for their debts and daily expenses; and the sixteenth being insufficient to afford us bread, we must live, as they now do, on oatmeal and potatoes; have no time to think, no means of calling the mismanagers to account; but be glad to obtain subsistence by hiring ourselves to rivet their chains on the necks of our fellow-sufferers.

—Thomas Jefferson, 1816

Issue #4

Robber Baron Capitalists

Statist Viewpoint

Controls on business people became necessary during the late 1800s because "robber baron[14] capitalists" were mistreating workers and charging unfair prices.

The Other Side of the Story

I urge you to read THE MYTH OF THE ROBBER BARONS by Burton W. Folsom, Jr. Americans are taught that the early industrialists were corrupt "robber barons" who charged unfair prices and wages until they were brought under control by the heroic U.S. Government. Folsom correctly shows that there were two groups of early industrialists. One was the monopolists who were indeed corrupt and were able to commit unforgivable abuses because the government was helping them do so. The other was the market entrepreneurs who had little or no connection with government and behaved honorably, helping improve the lot of workers and consumers alike.

---

[14] Robber baron. In the late 1800s, lawmakers granted special privileges to selected business owners and, in some cases, the business owners used these privileges to take unfair advantage of workers, consumers, and other businesses. These business owners came to be called robber baron capitalists. Persons commonly accused of being robber baron capitalists were Jay Gould, Cornelius Vanderbilt, Andrew Carnegie, J.P. Morgan and John D. Rockefeller.

In the absence of government privileges and subsidies, the only controls that are necessary are those provided naturally through the principles of common law and the forces of competition.

Notice the process used during the age of the robber barons. Statists handed out special privileges to a few, then when these privileges were abused, the statists used these abuses to argue that free markets do not work and controls must be levied on all of us.

What Would Thomas Jefferson Think About This?

Agriculture, manufactures, commerce and navigation, the four pillars of our prosperity, are the most thriving when left the most free to individual enterprise.

— Thomas Jefferson, 1801

Recommended Reading

- "Antitrust" by Alan Greenspan and "Notes on the History of American Free Enterprise" by Ayn Rand, both in the book CAPITALISM: THE UNKNOWN IDEAL by Ayn Rand. Published by Signet, Times Mirror, NY, 1966. For ages 15 and up.

- THE MYTH OF THE ROBBER BARONS by Burton W. Folsom, Jr. Published by Young America's Foundation, 110 Elden St., Ste. A, Herndon, VA 20170. For ages 14 and up.

Issue #5

"Governments Aren't Greedy"

Statist Viewpoint

Business people are motivated by greed and are not to be trusted. Government officials, on the other hand, are not greedy and can be trusted because they are selfless and motivated by a desire to protect and help us.

The Other Side of the Story

The statist viewpoint is rarely stated outright as I have done here, and you can see why. It's probably true that most people and organizations are motivated by greed to one extent or another, and it is abundantly true that governments are to a great extent. Every day your local newspaper is packed with announcements about businesses lowering their prices. When was the last time you got a break on your taxes?

Politicians and bureaucrats are as human as the rest of us and have all the same motivations and vices—except that they also have the privilege of satisfying their motivations and vices through the use of force.

**What Would
Thomas Jefferson
Think About This?**

Offices are as acceptable here as elsewhere, and whenever a man has cast a longing eye on them, a rottenness begins in his conduct.

—Thomas Jefferson, 1799

Recommended Viewing

- "Greed" by John Stossel. Produced by ABC News in 1998. Fifty minute documentary. Has also been available from Laissez Faire Books, phone: 800-326-0996 (http://LFB.com). For ages 14 and up.

Issue #6

Child Labor Laws

Statist Viewpoint

Child labor laws[15] were enacted to protect children from mistreatment by employers. These laws are good and necessary.

The Other Side of the Story

The issue is too complex to fully explain here but we can mention two points. (For an in-depth study refer to the recommended readings on the next page.)

First, a child who is suffering from sexual abuse or some other mistreatment cannot easily escape today because he or she cannot earn a living. Those who do escape end up wandering the streets and surviving through prostitution, theft, or other crime because they cannot get a legitimate job.

Second, the child labor laws have destroyed the apprentice system. Children cannot learn a trade and become independent as they did in past centuries. They are forced to remain children long past the age when their ancestors had become journeymen carpenters, mechanics, and tailors.

This isn't to say the very young should not be protected, it is only to say statist writers accept the so-called benefits of

---

[15] Child labor laws. Government regulations ostensibly enacted to protect children from harsh working conditions by forbidding the children to get jobs.

child labor laws without question and without examining the *hidden* costs.

Alternative Solution

Many states permit children to own and operate their own businesses.

Recommended Reading

- BETTER THAN A LEMONADE STAND! by Daryl Bernstein. Published by Beyond Words Publishing, Oregon. For ages 10 and up.

- CAPITALISM FOR KIDS by Karl Hess. Published by Bluestocking Press, phone: 800-959-8586, web site: www.BluestockingPress.com. For ages 10 and up.

- "The Effect of the Industrial Revolution on Women and Children" by Robert Hessen in CAPITALISM: THE UNKNOWN IDEAL by Ayn Rand (Chapter 8). Published by Signet, Times Mirror, NY, 1966. For ages 15 and up.

- "The Schools Ain't What They Used To Be and Never Was" in THE LIBERTARIAN ALTERNATIVE by Tibor Machan (Chapter 15). Published by Nelson Hall, Chicago, 1977. Out of print. For ages 16 and up.

- THE YOUNG ENTREPRENEUR'S GUIDE TO STARTING AND RUNNING A BUSINESS by Steve Mariotti. Published by Three Rivers Press, New York. For ages 13 and up.

Issue #7

Farmers Had Happier Lives

Statist Viewpoint

Before the Industrial Revolution,[16] life was better. People were happy and healthy living and working on farms. The Industrial Revolution locked them up in "dark satanic mills."

The Other Side of the Story

America is the only major nation that has never had a famine. The possibility of our children starving to death is so far outside the experience of most Americans that we have no comprehension of what life was like worldwide before 1776.

The mills of the early Industrial Revolution were grim by today's standards, but they were a vast improvement over anything that came before, and they boosted production and reduced prices of clothing and other essentials. A mill worker didn't worry about starving or freezing to death as most other workers did. The happy, healthy farm worker of pre-industrial times did not exist. Most were forever hungry, dirty, flea ridden, diseased, and barely a step ahead of the Grim Reaper.

---

[16] Industrial revolution. The period beginning in England around 1750 (and continuing today in more backward countries) when limited production of highly expensive goods by means of hand tools was replaced with mass production by heavy machinery and factories, leading to drastic reduction of prices and equally drastic increases in wages.

George Washington was part of America's upper class. When he was in his early teens he wrote 110 *Rules of Civility & Decent Behaviour in Company and Conversation* into his copybook. Rule #13:

> Kill no vermin as fleas, lice, ticks &c in the sight of others; if you see any filth or thick spittle, put your foot dexteriously upon it; if it be upon the clothes of your companions, put it off privately; and if it be upon your own clothes, return thanks to him who puts it off.

The early mills were no place a modern American would want to work, but the fact is that in most cases they were the best that could be done at that time and they saved the lives of the men, women, and children who worked there.

A book I dearly wish I could recommend is EVERYDAY LIFE THROUGH THE AGES (published by The Reader's Digest Association Limited, 1992). This beautifully illustrated and smoothly written volume is heavily researched and packed with fascinating information about the way humans lived in earlier times. This is history as it should be presented, with emphasis not on politics but on economics.

The books's fatal flaw is that much of its explanation of events has a strong statist slant echoing the myths commonly taught in schools and colleges throughout the United States. For instance, on page 271, the books says, "Hardship and poverty were widespread side effects of the Industrial Revolution." On page 269, the book laments the ten-hour shifts worked by women in Scottish coal mines.

Yet five pages earlier it correctly reports that in pre-industrial times, "men, women and children of entire villages—even of whole country towns—would be out in the fields, often working 16 hour days, and by moonlight if necessary," and "it was painful work." The book quotes the son of a farmer saying, "no one could stand the harvest-field as a reaper except he had been born to it." On page 150, it correctly reports that "Death and disease were no strangers to the filth-ridden towns and villages of medieval Europe." Few lived until old-age and famine was common. On page 271, after decrying the Industrial Revolution, the book even admits that in one English town "only 100 of the 9000 inhabitants were fully employed." These people were so poor that "many fasted every other day, or survived on boiled nettles."

In other words, the truth is that hardship and poverty were not caused by the Industrial Revolution, they existed long before it; the Industrial Revolution was the cure.

If the mills of the early Industrial Revolution were so terrible, why did workers in every nation leave their farms and flock to the cities to get jobs in these mills?

Recommended Reading

- FACTS ABOUT THE INDUSTRIAL REVOLUTION by Ludwig von Mises in FREE MARKET ECONOMICS, A BASIC READER by Bettina Bien Greaves. Published by the Foundation for Economic Education, Irvington-on-Hudson, NY. Out of print. For ages 15 and up.

What Would Thomas Jefferson Think About This?

I shall, therefore rejoin myself to my native country, with new attachments, and with exaggerated esteem for its advantages; for though there is less wealth there, there is more freedom, more ease, and less misery.

—Thomas Jefferson, 1785
(about his return to America from France)

Issue #8

Poverty and Crime

Statist Viewpoint
Poverty breeds crime.

The Other Side of the Story

"Poverty breeds crime" is one of the most corrosive and misleading statements in American culture today, and it's so pervasive it is rarely questioned.

"Poverty breeds crime" says to every poor person, "because you have a low income you are automatically disposed to being evil and brutal." How much hope can people have if they are continually receiving this message? Will they work hard to overcome their difficulties or will they just give up?

This viewpoint in particular is such a frustration because it is so clearly false. If poverty bred crime, then the 1930s Great Depression would have brought a crime wave of unimaginable proportions. Talk with anyone who remembers those times. They are likely to tell you about the "good old days" when they could leave their doors unlocked and safely walk their neighborhood streets at any time of the day or night.

HISTORICAL STATISTICS OF THE UNITED STATES: COLONIAL TIMES TO 1957, (U.S. Department of Commerce, 1961, pages 217 and 218) shows crime statistics indicating that the number of people going to prison during the Great Depression actually declined from previous years.

For all of history prior to the 20th century, everyone lived in poverty so grim we can hardly imagine it. Even royalty. They were continually threatened by scurvy because they had no fresh fruits in the winter. They had no good dental care or medical care. Most were illiterate. They had no electric lights, no hot or cold running water or indoor plumbing or eye glasses. In their wildest dreams they never imagined the "necessities" we take for granted: television, radio, telephones, computers, stereos, microwave ovens, refrigerators, central heating and air conditioning, cotton clothing, sunscreen lotion, automobiles, and on and on.

And that was royalty.

Try to grasp how awful it was for the common folk. Few lived as well as America's poorest do today.

Were all our ancestors criminals?

The wealthy royal families were criminals. Their wealth was acquired by forcibly taking it from others.

Granted, in previous centuries there were certain areas that were bad. For instance, no sane person would have wanted to spend much time in central Paris, France; Dodge City, Kansas; or Port Royal, Jamaica. But if poverty causes crime, then stealing and murder would have been the norm and civilization would have quickly collapsed long ago.

In 1940, teachers were surveyed about problems in the public schools. Compare their top problems with those cited by teachers in 1990:

1940 **Public School Problems**	1990 **Public School Problems**
Talking out of turn	Drug and alcohol abuse
Chewing gum	Pregnancy
Making noise	Suicide
Running in the halls	Rape
Cutting in line	Robbery
Dress code infractions	Assault[17]
Littering	

According to THE STATISTICAL ABSTRACT OF THE UNITED STATES, real (inflation-adjusted) median family income in 1990 was roughly three times that of 1940. So, why did the much poorer Americans of 1940 not have to worry about their children being raped, robbed, or assaulted in school?

If poverty causes crime, the schools of 1940 should have been war zones and those of today should be utopias.

This isn't to say poverty is a fine thing; it's terrible, but it does not cause crime.

Crime is not about poverty; it is about character. If there is crime in the poorer areas of our nation today, you can figure something is destroying the character of the people there.

---

[17] CQ RESEARCHER, September 11, 1993.

*According to our research crime is underesti-
mated by about 600%....we were unprepared for the
revelation that fully 60% or 600 in every 1000 adult
Americans have been the victim of at least one
crime....We further found that 350 in every 1000
Americans have been the victims of at least two
crimes.*

—James Patterson and Peter Kim
THE DAY AMERICA TOLD THE TRUTH

*According to the "National Survey of Adolescent
Alcohol, Tobacco, and Other Drug Use," PRIDE –
Drug Free Youth, 1997-98, during the 1997-98 school
year, 3.8% of 6th to 12th grade students (almost a
million students) reported they had carried a gun to
school.*

—Brady Center To Prevent Gun Violence
web site: http://www.bradycenter.org/stop2/facts/fs5.php

Issue #9

Wage-and-Price Spiral

Statist Viewpoint
The wage-and-price spiral[18] causes rising prices.

The Other Side of the Story
Rising prices are caused by inflation of the money supply. Inflation is not rising prices; it is an increase in the money supply, which causes rising prices. As the number of dollars increases, the value of each individual dollar falls and prices rise to compensate. Wages are the price of labor, so these prices rise, too.

---

[18] Wage-and-price spiral: the belief that unions demand higher wages, which pushes up the cost of production, which pushes up prices and creates pressure for more wage increases, and so on.

Recommended Reading and Listening

- THE GREAT ECONOMIC THINKERS, audio series produced by Knowledge Products, Nashville, TN. For ages 15 and up.

- THE INFLATION CRISIS AND HOW TO RESOLVE IT (formerly WHAT YOU SHOULD KNOW ABOUT INFLATION) by Henry Hazlitt. Contact the Foundation for Economic Education, Irvington-on-Hudson, NY. For ages 16 and up.

- THE CLIPPER SHIP STRATEGY, an Uncle Eric book, by Richard J. Maybury. Published by Bluestocking Press, web site : www.BluestockingPress.com, phone: 800-959-8586. For ages 14 and up.

- THE MONEY MYSTERY, an Uncle Eric book, by Richard J. Maybury. Published by Bluestocking Press, web site: www.BluestockingPress.com, phone: 800-959-8586. For ages 14 and up.

- WHATEVER HAPPENED TO PENNY CANDY?, an Uncle Eric book, by Richard J. Maybury. Published by Bluestocking Press, phone: 800-959-8586, web site: www.BluestockingPress.com. For ages 12 and up.

Issue #10

Needs of Society

Statist Viewpoint
The needs of society outweigh the needs of the individual.

The Other Side of the Story
Whenever someone starts talking about the needs of society, look out. The whole is not greater than the sum of its parts.

Society has no needs; only individuals have needs. Remove all the individuals and there is no society.

Beware of all collectivist terminology: "national interests," "social concerns," "social goods," "community needs," "public services." These fuzzy but high sounding phrases diminish the importance of the individual and serve as excuses to place more power in the hands of government officials. They set the stage for sacrificing the individual to the mob.

Recommended Reading

- CLICHES OF SOCIALISM by Leonard Read. Published by Foundation for Economic Education, Irvington-on-Hudson, NY. Out of print. For ages 14 and up.

What Would
Thomas Jefferson
Think About This?

The moral duties which exist between individual and individual in a state of nature, accompany them into a state of society, and the aggregate of the duties of all the individuals composing the society constitutes the duties of that society towards any other; so that between society and society the same moral duties exist as did between the individuals composing them, while in an unassociated state, and their maker not having released them from those duties on their forming themselves into a nation.

—Thomas Jefferson, 1793

Issue #11

Isolationism

Statist Viewpoint
Isolationism is bad.

The Other Side of the Story

In foreign policy, America's Founders believed our government should stay neutral but, as private individuals, Americans should travel, trade, and be friendly with everyone. Statists rarely talk about neutrality. They prefer to use the word isola-

> *The great rule of conduct for us, in regard to foreign nations is in extending our commercial relations, to have with them as little political connection as possible.*
>
> —George Washington, 1796

tionism. This gives the impression of Americans cutting themselves off from the rest of the world.

The other side of the story is that neutrality means: 1) recognizing that international problems are never so simple as good guys against bad guys as we are so often led to believe, and 2) having the self-control to not meddle in other people's affairs. Statists want the government involved in the affairs of other nations. This leads easily to war, the most exciting use of power.

See my two-part world war series[19] that explains America's entry into the two world wars and you will see the wisdom of the Founders' advice.

What Would
Thomas Jefferson
Think About This?

Commerce with all nations, alliance with none, should be our motto.

—Thomas Jefferson, 1799

We have a perfect horror at everything like connecting ourselves with the politics of Europe.

—Thomas Jefferson, 1801

I have ever deemed it fundamental for the United States, never to take active part in the quarrels of Europe. Their political interests are entirely distinct from ours...They are nations of eternal war.

—Thomas Jefferson, 1823

---

[19] Richard Maybury is referring to WORLD WAR I: THE REST OF THE STORY AND AND HOW IF AFFECTS YOU TODAY, and WORLD WAR II: THE REST OF THE STORY AND HOW IT AFFECTS YOU TODAY. Both are Uncle Eric books published by Bluestocking Press, phone: 800-959-8586, web site: www.BluestockingPress.com

Recommended Reading & Listening

- WORLD WAR I: THE REST OF THE STORY AND HOW IT AFFECTS YOU TODAY (1870 TO 1935), an Uncle Eric book, by Richard J. Maybury. Published by Bluestocking Press, phone: 800-959-8586, web site: www.BluestockingPress.com

- WORLD WAR II: THE REST OF THE STORY AND HOW IT AFFECTS YOU TODAY (1935 TO SEPTEMBER 11, 2001), an Uncle Eric book, by Richard J. Maybury. Published by Bluestocking Press, phone: 800-959-8586, web site: www.BluestockingPress.com

- THE FINAL SECRET OF PEARL HARBOR by Admiral Robert A. Theobald, USN Retired. Published by Devin-Adair, NY, 1954. Out of print. For ages 14 and up.

- "Free Societies and Foreign Affairs" in THE LIBERTARIAN ALTERNATIVE by Tibor Machan. (see section IV). Out of print. Published by Nelson Hall, Chicago. For ages 14 and up.

- UNITED STATES AT WAR audio history. Produced by Knowledge Products, Nashville, TN. For ages 14 and up.

- THE LIFE AND SELECTED WRITINGS OF THOMAS JEFFERSON, edited by Koch and Peden. See Jefferson's letters about war. Published by Random House, NY, 1972. For ages 15 and up.

Issue #12

Unions Saved Workers

Statist Viewpoint

Businesses refused to grant higher wages or better working conditions to workers until the workers formed unions[20] and forced these changes.

The Other Side of the Story

Unions did not bring better lighting to the factories, Thomas Edison did. A hundred years ago the new systems of scientific management found that workers produced more when they had better lighting, ventilation, and other amenities. As soon as these were invented, the more progressive businesses began using them to gain a competitive advantage over the less progressive businesses.

Unions do raise wages, but in so doing they also cause unemployment. An expensive worker is a worker likely to be replaced by a machine or some other innovation. If wages are forced up very much, the firm might even close down or move out of the country.

A worker with a $50,000 hydraulic backhoe can dig more ditches and earn higher wages than one with a $20 shovel. The only way to achieve a real, lasting improvement in wages

---

[20] Union: Short for labor union, or collective bargaining. A group of workers who band together and negotiate as a group, rather than individuals, for wages, benefits, and working conditions.

and working conditions is to accumulate the tools, training, raw materials, and other factors necessary for the workers themselves to be more *productive*. Unions have little to do with it, but they take the credit.

The best—some would say the only—real protection for workers is a free market in which employers must bid against each other for labor. Competition. Good workers will have a choice about taking their higher wages in the form of cash or in the form of health plans, pensions, or other benefits. Bad workers will have the choice of either earning bad wages or becoming better workers.

Unions have been helpful to workers, this is true. But the help has been exaggerated. If total costs of unions, hidden as well as unhidden, were weighted against total benefits, we would see a picture much different than the one most of us have been taught.

Recommended Reading

- "Labor, Wages and Employment" in FREE MARKET ECONOMICS, A BASIC READER, by Bettina Bien Greaves. Published by the Foundation for Economic Education. Out of print. For ages 13 and up.

Issue #13

Social Security is Beneficial

Statist Viewpoint

Social Security[21] is a wonderful example of "social engineering" by government to relieve hardship.

The Other Side of the Story

We don't hear this statist viewpoint much any more, even the most dedicated statist now realizes Social Security is really just a gigantic Ponzi scheme that is impoverishing the young. As such, it is a wonderful example of government's social engineering.

Named after swindler Charles Ponzi, a Ponzi scheme is a pyramid scam like a chain letter. Investors are paid not from their investment's earnings but from the money poured in by new investors. Ponzi schemes are inherently unstable and they eventually go broke.

---

[21] Social Security: A government program that provides money and other assistance to persons who are retired or disabled, financed by taxes on those who are not retired or disabled.

Recommended Reading

- "Burden for Grandchildren" in WALL STREET JOURNAL, 9 April 1991, p. 18. For ages 15 and up.

- "Generation War" in NEWSWEEK, 10 February 1992, p. 8. For ages 15 and up.

- "Sixtysomething" in U.S. NEWS AND WORLD REPORT, 23 April 1990, p. 80; and 14 May 1990, p. 82. For ages 15 and up.

- "Social Security" in WALL STREET JOURNAL, 15 January 1990, p. 1. For ages 15 and up.

- Speech by Commissioner of Social Security John A. Svahn, VITAL SPEECHES OF THE DAY, 1 September 1982. For ages 15 and up.

- "Social Security and Its Discontents," by economist John Attarian, THE WORLD AND I magazine, January 2003, p. 251.

- The Cato Project on Social Security, Cato Institute, www.cato.org

Issue #14

War

Statist Viewpoint
War is good for the economy.

The Other Side of the Story
Of all the half-truths commonly taught, this must be the most vicious. The economy is not a machine, it is people; killing people is not good for them.

Even those who are not killed or wounded usually suffer. Wars bring higher taxes, inflation, shortages, dislocations, and massive malinvestment; they are followed by recessions and depressions.

Some persons do benefit. Firms and their employees who make weapons earn more money, but they are only a small part of the population, seldom more than ten percent.

War does tend to reduce unemployment to some extent. Everyone who wants a job can find one because of the boom caused by inflation of the money supply. Also, some who would otherwise be unemployed are killed.

Government always profits from war. Government emerges from war larger and more powerful. War is generally the most effective way for government to grow.

But on balance for the nation as a whole, war is always a catastrophe. It is the most expensive and destructive thing humans do. Any alternative is cheaper.

This isn't to say we should not defend our homes and families. We should, certainly—if we are sure the threat to our homes and families is real and not a made up excuse for statists to gather more power. But the war will not be good for the economy.

What Would Thomas Jefferson Think About This?

Never was so much false arithmetic employed on any subject, as that which has been employed to persuade nations that it is in their interest to go to war.

—Thomas Jefferson

Recommended Listening, Reading, and Viewing

- AMERICANIZATION OF EMILY. Film starring James Garner and Julie Andrews (1964). U.S. admiral plans to have American naval officer become the first casualty on Normandy at start of the invasion. Parental discretion advised.

- BLACK HAWK DOWN. Film starring Josh Hartnett (2002). Dramatizes the 1993 U.S. military mission in Somalia. Graphically violent. Rated R. For ages 17 and up.

- WE WERE SOLDIERS. Film starring Mel Gibson (2002). Story of first soldiers led into battle in Vietnam in 1965. Graphically violent. Rated R. For ages 17 and up.

- THOUSAND YEAR WAR IN THE MIDEAST, WORLD WAR I, WORLD WAR II. All three Uncle Eric books by Richard J. Maybury give the other side of the story about war. Published by Bluestocking Press, web site: www.BluestockingPress.com, phone: 800-959-8586.

- UNITED STATES AT WAR. Audio history series spanning pre-American Revolution through the Vietnam War. Narrated by George C. Scott. Produced by Knowledge Products, Nashville, TN. For ages 14 and up.

Issue #15

Sacrifice

Statist Viewpoint

Sacrifice means loss, and sacrifice is good, so loss is good and profit is bad.

The Other Side of the Story

When Jesus Christ died on the cross, did he do it for nothing?[22]

He was trying to achieve something he wanted. He was expending something valuable, his life, in hopes of accomplishing something he valued more. He was seeking a gain. We can ask the same question about Abraham, Mohammed, and other religious figures, as well as more current heroes who made great sacrifices, such as Gandhi, Mother Teresa, and Sergeant York. Did they do it for nothing, or were they trying to achieve something?

The meaning of the word sacrifice has been changed. Originally sacrifice meant investment. You made an expenditure or took a risk in hopes it would lead to a profit of some kind. In the story of Cain and Abel, sacrifices were made to gain favor with God.

Today sacrifice means doing something without expectation of gain. We are supposed to feel good about doing for

---

[22] My thanks to friend Barry Conner for contributing this insight.

others, but feel guilty about doing for ourselves. Movies and books make heroes of persons who suffer losses — and villains of persons who prosper. The wealthy industrialist has become the all-purpose bad guy.

Part of this change in the meaning of sacrifice is due to the false economic assumption that life is a zero sum game. In a zero sum game, for one person to win another must lose.

In a free market controlled by common law and the forces of competition, both parties in a transaction can earn a profit. (For a more detailed study of this, read Karl Hess's CAPITALISM FOR KIDS and Ayn Rand's CAPITALISM: THE UNKNOWN IDEAL.)

Recommended Reading

- CAPITALISM FOR KIDS by Karl Hess. Published by Bluestocking Press, phone: 800-959-8586, web site: www.BluestockingPress.com

- CAPITALISM: THE UNKNOWN IDEAL by Ayn Rand. Published by Signet, Times Mirror, NY, 1966. For ages 15 and up.

- CLICHES OF SOCIALISM by Leonard Read. Published by Foundation for Economic Education, Irvington-on-Hudson, NY. Out of print. For ages 14 and up.

- WHATEVER HAPPENED TO JUSTICE? (chapters 10 and 11), an Uncle Eric book, by Richard J. Maybury. Published by Bluestocking Press, web site: www.BluestockingPress.com, phone: 800-959-8586

Issue #16

The Founders'
Motives Were Corrupt

Statist Viewpoint

The American Revolution was not about liberty. America's Founders were corrupt, they launched the revolution to profit from it.

The Other Side of the Story

Many books about American history attempt to discredit the Founders by claiming they led the revolution for personal gain.

Three points. First, doing something for personal gain does not make it dishonorable.

Second, when one person gains, this does not mean others must lose. It is entirely possible for one person to do something for personal gain and, in the process, accomplish ends that benefit many.

Third, the Founders risked their lives and some suffered horribly in the revolution exposing themselves to direct enemy fire.

In a small cemetery at Berkeley Plantation on Virginia's James River is a tablet with the following inscription:

By signing the Declaration of Independence, the 56 Americans pledged their lives, their fortunes and their sacred honor.

It was no idle pledge.

Nine signers died of wounds during the Revolutionary War.

Five signers were captured or imprisoned.

Wives, children were killed, jailed, mistreated or left penniless.

Twelve signers' houses were burned to the ground.

Seventeen signers lost everything they owned.

No signers defected.

Their honor, like their country, remained intact.

Did they do it for personal gain? Yes, they made the sacrifice in hopes of acquiring a better life for themselves, their families, and their country.

What Would Thomas Jefferson Think About This?

And for the support of this declaration, with a firm reliance on the protection of divine providence, we mutually pledge to each other our lives, our fortunes, and our sacred honor.

— Thomas Jefferson
Declaration of Independence

Misleading Terms

Watch for these misleading terms:

- **Debt to society.** Society does not exist, only individuals
exist. Take away all the individuals and there is no society.
Someone who sets out to pay his debt to "society" usually
ends up paying the government.

- **Democracy.** Democracy is majority rule but it is often
used to mean liberty. In reality, democracy is one of the
most serious threats to liberty. America was founded as a
federation and a republic, not a democracy. A federation
is a group of states joined together in an alliance, mostly
for shared military protection. A republic is a government
in which the people vote for representatives who go to the
capitol and vote according to what the representatives
believe is best, not necessarily what the voters want. (See
WHATEVER HAPPENED TO JUSTICE?, an Uncle Eric book, by
Richard J. Maybury published by Bluestocking Press.)

- **The economy.** This term is used by virtually all writers,
so you must watch closely to see how it is used. "The
economy" is seen by statists and other powerseekers as a
kind of machine that can be adjusted or "fine tuned." In
reality, the economy is a kind of ecology made of biologi-
cal organisms—humans. Trying to fine tune or adjust
them tends to damage them in the same way as fine-tuning
or adjusting a coral reef or a rain forest would damage
them. Humans do not know enough, and probably never

will, to be able to improve something so unimaginably complex. A single cell of a living organism, for instance, is much too complex for mere mortals to fully understand, and each living organism is composed of millions of cells.

- **Germany invaded Poland.** We are forever hearing about Germany doing this, Britain doing that, or Russia or the U.S. doing something else. In the case of "Germany did this," the fact is that specific German officials did it—as is the case in all nations. All Germans are not involved— many may be completely opposed to the act—and so forth for all nations. By referring to governments as if they were entire nations, we collectivize guilt and set the stage to punish all the citizens for the actions of a few. This is one of the main causes of war. For a good insight into the ways collectivized guilt prolonged the Second World War read UNCONDITIONAL SURRENDER (published by Rutger's University, out of print—check your library) by historian Anne Armstrong. Armstrong shows that the Allies refused to acknowledge that many Germans hated Hitler and were trying to kill him; when these Germans asked for help, the Allies ignored them. The Allies' assumption that they were fighting "Germany" instead of specific Germans prolonged the war and led to millions of needless deaths. Another excellent book is HITLER'S GERMAN ENEMIES by Louis L. Snyder, published by Hippocrene Books, NY, 1990. This book gives the anti-Hitler German side of the story (for ages 15 and up).

- **Interests.** There was a day when United States troops were expected to fight and die for liberty. Now it's interests. Some presidents use the term vital interests, and others national interests; some just say interests.

For two centuries, American troops have been sent all over the world to meddle in other countries and risk their lives for our "interests." In his 1989 inaugural address, President George H. W. Bush echoed a parade of presidents, both Democratic and Republican, saying, "We will defend our allies and our interests."

No one ever explains what an interest is or why it is worth dying for. Nowhere is there a war memorial inscribed with, "They Gave Their Lives For Our National Interests." Nowhere in the Constitution is the word interests defined.

But we know where the term came from. The Roman Senate declared that emperor Vespasian "shall have the right...to do whatever he deems to serve the interests of the state."

In other words, interests means carte blanche to do anything to anyone—because it is for our interests.

- **Patriotism.** Suppose the government is harming the country, and you resist. Are you being a traitor, or a patriot?

   When America's Founders were trying to overthrow their government and establish a new nation, the soldiers sometimes became disheartened by the overwhelming difficulty of the task. In the freezing winter of 1776-77, George Washington ordered that Thomas Paine's new pamphlet THE AMERICAN CRISIS be read to his soldiers. The pamphlet began: "These are the times that try men's souls. The summer soldier and the sunshine patriot will, in this crisis, shrink from the service of his country; but he that stands it now, deserves the love and thanks of man and woman. Tyranny, like hell, is not easily conquered." The government was overthrown, and the new nation established.

Statists sometimes get control of the government and use patriotism as their excuse for doing harm to the country. "Patriotism is the last refuge of a scoundrel," said the great English lexicographer Samuel Johnson.

Sometimes statists are able to rally the nation behind their cause. "When a whole nation is roaring Patriotism at the top of its voice, I am fain[23] to explore the cleanness of its hands and purity of its heart," wrote Ralph Waldo Emerson.

Mark Twain summed up the American view of patriotism: "My kind of loyalty was loyalty to one's country, not to its institutions or its officeholders."

If you remain dedicated to the *principles* on which America was founded, you'll be the kind of patriot Thomas Jefferson and the other Founders admired.

- **Republic.** America was founded as a federation and a republic, not a democracy. A federation is a group of states joined together in an alliance, mostly for shared military protection. A republic is a government in which the people vote for representatives who go to the capitol and vote according to what the representatives believe is best, not necessarily what the voters want. (See WHATEVER HAPPENED TO JUSTICE?, an Uncle Eric book, by Richard J. Maybury published by Bluestocking Press.)

- **Rights** (also Entitlements). Under the old common law our rights were limited and clearly defined. You had the God-given right to be secure in your life, liberty, and property, no one was allowed to encroach.

---

[23] compelled.

Today we have a "right" to education, a "right" to medical care, a "right" to food, clothing, and shelter. One person's right is another person's obligation. If I have a right to all these benefits, then someone else is obligated to provide them for me. This someone is, therefore, my slave.

- **Social Justice** (also Social Equity) This is one of the most cleverly misleading terms in use today. It's so similar to the old common law word "justice" that persons who believe in liberty are easily misled into voting for it and, therefore, voting for more statism.

  Social justice means using political power to rob Peter to subsidize Paul. Generally, statists who speak of social justice are hoping power will be used to "level" society, meaning to take from haves and give to have-nots. The scheme always sounds so attractive, especially to have-nots, but in the real world it leads inexorably to higher taxes, more powerful bureaucracies, slower economic development, and unemployment.

  There is a reason most religions forbid us to covet our neighbor's goods, and there is a reason many persons who believe in "social justice" so often speak ill of religion.

- **Unregulated.** This word, although it literally means free, is used by statists as an automatic indictment. Powerseekers believe anything that is unregulated by government is bad. They give no consideration to the fact that common law and the forces of competition are by far the most effective form of regulation, if they are allowed to operate. Government regulation often stifles competition and common law and creates unfair advantages.

Politics Has Become Religion

When discussing politics, history, or economics, bear in mind that many Americans have been unknowingly steeped in statism to the point that government has become their de facto god. It is their source of security and the solution to their problems. They have faith in it.

To challenge their politics is to challenge their religion, which can be emotionally unsettling for them.

Further, it can put you in the position of being a heretic,[24] and heretics are often treated unkindly.

When in the presence of statism, go carefully, these are deep waters.

---

[24] Heretic. A person who disagrees with accepted beliefs.

Positive Indicators

The indicators listed in the following section show that a book agrees with the original American philosophy.

Make notes while the indicators are fresh in your mind. Compile your own list of books that agree with the indicator. (More of my own favorite books are listed in WHATEVER HAPPENED TO PENNY CANDY? and WHATEVER HAPPENED TO JUSTICE?)

Positive Indicator #1

Quality of Life

When a book reveals or discusses the amazing advancement in the quality of life in America since 1776, this is a good sign. This advancement has been due almost entirely to industrial capitalism which was made possible by the common law principles of the American Revolution.

A book that contrasts human life before and after 1776 is rare and wonderful.

Recommended Reading

- CAPITALISM AND THE HISTORIANS edited by F.A. Hayek. Published by the University of Chicago Press, 1954. For ages 15 and up.

- DISCOVERY OF FREEDOM by Rose Wilder Lane. Published by Fox & Wilkes, San Francisco, CA. For ages 14 and up.

- GIVE ME LIBERTY by Rose Wilder Lane. Out of print. For ages 14 and up.

- "Facts about the Industrial Revolution" by Ludwig von Mises in FREE MARKET ECONOMICS: A BASIC READER by Bettina Bien Greaves. Published by Foundation for Economic Education, Irvington-on-Hudson, New York. Out of print. For ages 14 and up.

- LITTLE HOUSE BOOKS by Laura Ingalls Wilder. Published by Harper Collins, NY. For ages 7 and up.

- MAINSPRING OF HUMAN PROGRESS by Henry Grady Weaver. Published by Foundation for Economic Education, Irvington-on-Hudson, New York. For ages 14 and up.

Positive Indicator #2

Individualism

When a book celebrates individualism, independent thinking, or exposes the irrationality of crowds, this is a very hopeful sign.

Recommended Reading and Listening

- THE ANTI-FEDERALIST PAPERS AND THE CONSTITU-TIONAL CONVENTION DEBATES edited by Ralph Ketcham. Published by Mentor Books, NY. For ages 15 and up.

- THE ENTERPRISING AMERICANS by John Chamberlain. Published by Institute for Christian Economics, TX. Out of print. For ages 15 and up.

- ESSAYS ON INDIVIDUALITY edited by Felix Morley. Published by Liberty Fund, Inc., Indianapolis, 1977. Out of print. For ages 15 and up.

- EXTRAORDINARY POPULAR DELUSIONS AND THE MAD-NESS OF CROWDS by Charles Mackay. Published by Three Rivers Press, a division of Random House. New York. For ages 15 and up.

- THE FEDERALIST PAPERS by Hamilton, Madison, and Jay. Published by Mentor Books, NY. For ages 15 and up.

- THE FEDERALIST PAPERS. Audio produced by Knowledge Products, Nashville, TN. For ages 14 and up.

Positive Indicator #3

Accomplishment Deserves Reward

When a book assumes or, better yet, explicitly teaches that an individual should be rewarded for his accomplishments, this is a hopeful sign.

Recommended Reading

- CAPITALISM FOR KIDS: GROWING UP TO BE YOUR OWN BOSS by Karl Hess. Published by Bluestocking Press, web site: www.BluestockingPress.com, phone 800-959-8586. For ages 9 and up.

- DISCOVERY OF FREEDOM by Rose Wilder Lane. Published by Fox & Wilkes, San Francisco, CA. For ages 14 and up.

- GIVE ME LIBERTY by Rose Wilder Lane. Out of print. For ages 14 and up.

- MAINSPRING OF HUMAN PROGRESS by Henry Grady Weaver. Published by Foundation for Economic Education, Irvington-on-Hudson, New York. For ages 14 and up.

- ROOTS OF CAPITALISM by John Chamberlain. Published by Liberty Fund, Inc., Indianapolis, IN, 1977. For ages 15 and up.

Positive Indicator #4

Higher Law Exists

A book that assumes there is a Higher Law than any human law will be a rare gem.

Recommended Reading

- "The American Contribution" in the CONSTITUTION OF LIBERTY by F.A. Hayek (see chapter 12). Published by the University of Chicago Press, 1960. For ages 17 and up.

- Religious books, depending on your personal beliefs.

- THE DRINKING GOURD by F. N. Monjo. Published by Harper Collins, NY. For ages 4-8.

- LITTLE TOWN ON THE PRAIRIE (see chapter 8, "Fourth of July") by Laura Ingalls Wilder. Published by Harper Collins, NY. For ages 7 and up.

- THE REVOLUTIONARY YEARS, by Mortimer Adler. Published by Encyclopedia Britannica, Chicago, 1976. Out of print. For ages 16 and up.

- JONATHAN MAYHEW'S SERMON. Available through Bluestocking Press, phone: 800-959-8586, web site: www.BluestockingPress.com. For ages 14 and up.

Recommended Viewing

- JUDGMENT AT NUREMBERG. Film starring Spencer Tracy. The Nuremberg trials and the choices judges made.

Positive Indicator #5

Heroes Use Brain Not Brawn

Search for books that have heroes who are resourceful problem solvers rather than action figures. The emphasis should be on intelligence — not power.

Recommended Reading

- ALISTAIR COOKE'S AMERICA by Alistair Cooke. Published by Alfred A. Knopf, NY, 1973. Out of print. For ages 14 and up.

- Biographies of Thomas Edison and other inventors and scientists.

- CONNECTIONS by James Burke. Published by Little, Brown & Co., MA, 1978. Out of print. For ages 14 and up.

- THE ENTERPRISING AMERICANS by John Chamberlain. Published by Institute for Christian Economics, TX. Out of print. For ages 15 and up.

- THE HARDY BOYS, TOM SWIFT, and NANCY DREW books. Original edition. Published by Applewood Books, MA. For ages 10 and up.

- LITTLE HOUSE BOOKS by Laura Ingalls Wilder. Published by Harper Collins, NY. For ages 7 and up.

- LUDWIG VON MISES: SCHOLAR, CREATOR, HERO by Murray N. Rothbard (1988). Published by the Ludwig von Mises Institute, 518 West Magnolia Ave., Auburn, AL, 36832, ph: 334-321-2100, web site: www.mises.org. For ages 16 and up.

Positive Indicator #6

Evidence vs. Opinion

A book should emphasize the overwhelming importance of rational thought. The reader should be encouraged to seek *evidence* and to examine this evidence logically and dispassionately. A measurement should carry more weight than the opinion of the largest crowd.

Hoaxes abound, and some are astoundingly popular even among learned scholars who ought to know better. Perhaps the most valuable defense you can teach your child is the habit of asking "Where is the evidence?" and to require that this evidence be measurable and verifiable.

Recommended Reading

- ADVENTURES OF SHERLOCK HOLMES (all stories) by Arthur Conan Doyle. Variety of publishers. For ages 13 and up.

- CAPITALISM AND THE HISTORIANS edited by F.A. Hayek. Published by University of Chicago Press, 1963. For ages 14 and up.

- COSMOS by Carl Sagan. Published by Random House, 1980. For ages 13 and up.

- ECONOMICS ON TRIAL by Mark Skousen. Published by Irwin Professional Publishing, Burr Ridge, IL. Out of print. For ages 16 and up.

- STAR TREK stories featuring the characters of Spock or Data. Variety of publishers. Ages 12 and up.

- TODAY AND TOMORROW AND... by Isaac Asimov. Published by Dell, NY, 1973. For ages 13 and up.

Positive Indicator #7

Objective Truth

Right and wrong are not matters of opinion. They may be difficult to discover but they do exist and they cannot be made up.

Recommended Reading

• Religious books, depending on your personal beliefs.

• THE CONSTITUTION OF LIBERTY by F.A. Hayek. Published by University of Chicago Press, IL. For ages 16 and up.

• LITTLE TOWN ON THE PRAIRIE by Laura Ingalls Wilder. Published by Harper Collins, NY. For ages 7 and up.

• ORIGINS OF THE COMMON LAW by Arthur R. Hogue. Published by Liberty Press, Indianapolis, IN. 1966. For ages 16 and up.

• PLANNED CHAOS by Ludwig von Mises. Published by the Foundation for Economic Education, Irvington-on-Hudson, NY, 1947. For ages 16 and up.

• WHATEVER HAPPENED TO JUSTICE?, an Uncle Eric book, by Richard J. Maybury. Published by Bluestocking Press, phone: 800-959-8586, web site: www.BluestockingPress.com. For ages 12 and up.

Positive Indicator #8

Tanstaafl

When describing benefits of government programs, a book should also give detailed, *quantified* descriptions of all costs and risks, including those that are hidden, and the persons who are bearing these costs and risks. Tanstaafl: There Ain't No Such Thing As A Free Lunch.

Recommended Reading

- "Economic Teaching at the Universities" in PLAN-NING FOR FREEDOM by Ludwig von Mises (see Chapter 11). Published by Libertarian Press, South Holland, IL, 1974. For ages 17 and up.

- ECONOMICS IN ONE LESSON by Henry Hazlitt. Published by Crown, NY. For ages 15 and up.

- ECONOMICS ON TRIAL by Mark Skousen. Published by Irwin Professional Publishing, Burr Ridge, IL. Out of print. For ages 16 and up.

- "Tanstaafl, the Romans, and Us" in WHATEVER HAPPENED TO PENNY CANDY? 5th edition, an Uncle Eric book, by Richard J. Maybury. Published by Bluestocking Press, phone: 800-959-8586, web site: www.BluestockingPress.com. For ages 10 and up.

Positive Indicator #9

Overcome Problems
and Move Forward

Perhaps more than anything else, a book should assume humans have the ability to overcome their problems and move forward. Believe it or not, a popular theme in novels today is that all is lost, there is no hope, the individual is helpless.

One of the most noteworthy characteristics of America's Founders is that they were aware their own world, and indeed their own characters and personalities, were not the best that humans could do. They worried about slavery, poverty, and war and wanted something better. More importantly, they knew enough law and economics to believe something better was possible and they were working toward this goal.

They were not utopians. They realized a perfect society is not possible. But they knew we could do much better, and they were trying to create the legal environment that would enable this to happen.

After the battles of Lexington and Concord, Thomas Paine wrote COMMON SENSE. This generated support for overthrow of the government and the Declaration of Independence. COMMON SENSE was probably the most important and popular work ever published in America; George Washington referred to its "sound doctrine and unanswerable reasoning." In it Paine wrote of the revolution and the better world to come:

'Tis not the concern of a day, a year, or an age; posterity are virtually involved in the contest and will be more or less affected even to the end of time by the proceedings now...

O! ye that love mankind! Ye that dare oppose not only the tyranny but the tyrant, stand forth! Every spot of the Old World is overrun with oppression. Freedom has been hunted round the globe. Asia and Africa have long expelled her. Europe regards her as a stranger, and England has given her warning to depart. O! receive the fugitive, and prepare in time an asylum[25] for mankind.

The belief that a better tomorrow is possible is absolutely essential, not only for the rescue of our country but for the mental well-being of the individual. Young people need it desperately.

However, we need to *visualize* this better future, and few of us have imaginations fertile enough to do this alone. We need writers of literature to help us.

This is why I recommend, with parental discretion, the STAR TREK stories. For the most part, STAR TREK is well thought out and places great emphasis on the need for logic and evidence.

The "Prime Directive," which is a centerpiece of the STAR TREK world, is straight from original American principles. All the starship's crewmembers voluntarily take an oath to obey this rule which forbids them to encroach on others.

---

[25] refuge

STAR TREK books and scripts are not of the caliber of Shakespeare or Mark Twain, and issues from specific episodes may be inconsistent with a family's own belief system, but much of it is good and it provides the hope we need so much. I encourage you to watch with your children. Many episodes can lead to deeper discussions within the family.

Recommended Reading

- THE ENTERPRISING AMERICANS by Chamberlain. Published by Institute for Christian Economics, TX. For ages 15 and up.

- EXPLORING THE EARTH AND COSMOS by Isaac Asimov. Published by Crown, NY, 1982. Out of print. For ages 15 and up.

- FREE LAND (University of Nebraska Press) and LET THE HURRICANE ROAR (out of print) by Rose Wilder Lane. Ages 14 and up.

- THE GIRL WHO OWNED A CITY by O.T. Nelson. Published by Dell Laurel-Leaf, NY. For ages 10 and up.

- ISLAND OF THE BLUE DOLPHINS by Scott O'dell. Published by Bantam Doubleday Dell, NY. For ages 10 and up.

- JULIE OF THE WOLVES by Jean Craighead George. Published by Harper Collins, NY. For ages 13 and up.

- LITTLE HOUSE BOOKS by Laura Ingalls Wilder. Published by Harper Collins, NY. For ages 7 and up.

- ROBINSON CRUSOE by Daniel Defoe. Published by Signet, NY, 1961. For ages 13 and up.

- ROUGHING IT and LIFE ON THE MISSISSIPPI by Mark Twain. Published by Bantam, NY, 1960. For ages 14 and up.

- WISDOM OF ADAM SMITH by Benjamin Rogge. Published by Liberty Press, Indianapolis, 1976. For ages 15 and up.

- YOUNG INDIANA JONES.™ Published by Random House, NY. For ages 10 and up.

Examples

To get you started reading information consistent with the principles of America's Founders, here are three articles written by Richard Maybury that originally appeared in THE FREE MARKET newsletter published by the Mises Institute and reprinted with permission.[26]

The articles are about American history.

Following these articles is a list of authors whose work is generally consistent with the principles of America's Founders.

---

[26] Ludwig von Mises Institute, 518 West Magnolia Ave., Auburn, AL, 36832, ph: 800-636-4737, 334-321-2100, web site: www.mises.org.

The Great Thanksgiving Hoax[27]

By Richard J. Maybury

Each year at this time school children all over America are taught the official Thanksgiving story, and newspapers, radio, TV, and magazines devote vast amounts of time and space to it. It is all very colorful and fascinating.

It is also very deceiving. This official story is nothing like what really happened. It is a fairy tale, a whitewashed and sanitized collection of half-truths which divert attention away from Thanksgiving's real meaning.

The official story has the Pilgrims boarding the May-flower, coming to America, and establishing the Plymouth colony in the winter of 1620-21. This first winter is hard and half the colonists die. But the survivors are hard working and tenacious, and they learn new farming techniques from the Indians. The harvest of 1621 is bountiful. The Pilgrims hold a celebration and give thanks to God. They are grateful for the wonderful new abundant land He has given them.

The official story then has the Pilgrims living more or less happily ever after, each year repeating the first Thanksgiving. Other early colonies also have hard times at first, but they soon prosper and adopt the annual tradition of giving thanks for this prosperous new land called America.

---

[27] Reprinted with permission from THE FREE MARKET, November 1985 issue, published by the Ludwig von Mises Institute, 518 West Magnolia Ave., Auburn, AL, 36832, ph: 800-636-4737, 334-321-2100, web site: www.mises.org.

The problem with this official story is that the harvest of 1621 was not bountiful, nor were the colonists hardworking or tenacious. Sixteen hundred and twenty-one (1621) was a famine year and many of the colonists were lazy thieves. In his HISTORY OF PLYMOUTH PLANTATION, the governor of the colony, William Bradford, reported that the colonists went hungry for years because they refused to work in the fields. They preferred instead to steal food. He says the colony was riddled with "corruption" and with "confusion and discontent." The crops were small because "much was stolen both by night and day, before it became scarce eatable."

In the harvest feasts of 1621 and 1622, "all had their hungry bellies filled," but only briefly. The prevailing condition during those years was not the abundance the official story claims, it was famine and death. The first "Thanksgiving" was not so much a celebration as it was the last meal of condemned men.

But in subsequent years something changes. The harvest of 1623 was different. Suddenly, "instead of famine now God gave them plenty," Bradford wrote, "and the face of things was changed, to the rejoicing of the hearts of many, for which they blessed God." Thereafter, he wrote, "any general want or famine hath not been amongst them since to this day." In fact, in 1624, so much food was produced that the colonists were able to begin *exporting* corn.

What happened?

After the poor harvest of 1622, writes Bradford, "they began to think how they might raise as much corn as they could, and obtain a better crop." They began to question their form of economic organization.

This had required that "all profits & benefits that are got by trade, traffic, trucking, working, fishing, or any other means" were to be placed in the common stock of the colony, and that, "all such persons as are of this colony, are to have their meat, drink, apparel, and all provisions out of the common stock." A person was to put into the common stock all he could, and take only what he needed.

This "from each according to his ability, to each according to his need" was an early form of socialism, and it is why the Pilgrims were starving. Bradford writes that "young men that were most able and fit for labor and service" complained about being forced to "spend their time and strength to work for other men's wives and children." Also, "the strong, or man of parts, had no more in division of victuals and clothes, than he that was weak." So the young and strong refused to work and the total amount of food produced was never adequate.

To rectify this situation, in 1623 Bradford abolished socialism. He gave each household a parcel of land and told them they could keep what they produced or trade it away as they saw fit. In other words, he replaced socialism with a free market and that was the end of the famines.

Many early groups of colonists set up socialist states, all with the same terrible results. At Jamestown, established in 1607, out of every shipload of settlers that arrived, less than half would survive their first twelve months in America. Most of the work was being done by only one-fifth of the men, the other four-fifths choosing to be parasites. In the winter of 1609-10, called "The Starving Time," the population fell from five-hundred to sixty.

Then the Jamestown colony was converted to a free market, and the results were every bit as dramatic as those at Plymouth. In 1614, Colony Secretary Ralph Hamor wrote that after the switch there was "plenty of food, which every man by his own industry may easily and doth procure." He said that when the socialist system had prevailed, "we reaped not so much corn from the labors of thirty men as three men have done for themselves now."

Before these free markets were established, the colonists had nothing for which to be thankful. They were in the same situation as Ethiopians are today and for the same reasons. But after free markets were established, the resulting abundance was so dramatic that annual Thanksgiving celebrations became common throughout the colonies and, in 1863, Thanksgiving became a national holiday.

Thus the real meaning of Thanksgiving, deleted from the official story, is: Socialism does not work; the one and only source of abundance is free markets, and we thank God we live in a country where we can have them.

A Tribute to the Statue of Ellis Island[28]

by Richard Maybury

(This is a satire written in 1986 to give the correct history of the Statue of Liberty.)

December 31, 1999

Today as we enter the 21st Century we should pay tribute to the Statue of Ellis Island. This grand symbol of our government's power and majesty was not always so grand. Only twenty years ago the Lady was a broken, corroded heap of copper and iron. Even her name, Liberty Enlightening the World, was outdated, nearly forgotten, and seriously in need of modernization. The old makes way for the new, it has always been so.

But before we embrace the new — before we enter the next century — let's briefly look back at the long and difficult journey our nation and this lady have traveled together. We will never pass this way again.

The journey originated in the Middle Ages. During those terrible grim centuries, people were uneducated and they did

---

[28] This article by Richard Maybury originally appeared in THE FREE MARKET, March 1986 issue, published by the Ludwig von Mises Institute, 518 West Magnolia Ave., Auburn, AL, 36832, ph: 800-636-4737, 334-321-2100, web site: www.mises.org. It is reprinted with permission.

not yet understand the beauty of political power. Many thought it wrong to have a government empowered to legislate—that is, empowered to make whatever laws appear necessary without regard to moral principles or other idealistic nonsense.

Instead these poor wretches labored under the mistaken assumption that laws should change rarely and only when logically consistent with basic moral principles. A strange legal system called common law began to develop.

This ludicrous system was based on the two fundamental laws common to all major religions, philosophies, and other superstitions. These laws were: 1) do all you have agreed to do, and 2) do not encroach on other persons or their property.

Century after century, common law evolved. Government officials knew it was degenerative and they tried to alter or abolish it, but the ignorant common folk clung to their superstitions.

Then, during the 1600s, shipbuilding technology advanced to the point that many individuals could escape to America, beyond the reach of their government. They hoped to live under common law only, without benefit of legislative law.

A curious and greatly misunderstood chain of events then occurred, and these events produced both our country and our Lady.

Since the common law changed only slowly, and mostly in ways consistent with the two fundamental laws, the Americans found they were able to *plan ahead* in their work, investment, and trade. Their stable legal environment produced what was known in 1776 as "The System of Natural Liberty." Incorporating what economists call "effective economic calculation," this system was the free market.

For a while the free market seemed to produce considerable abundance for the common people. Poverty declined and America became the most prosperous land ever known.

Then during the 1760s, government officials became concerned about our forefather's contempt for authority. They tried to levy the taxes and regulations that would make Americans accustomed to legislative law.

Our forefathers became angry and violent. The 1776 revolution brought a split from England and a new nation founded in the principles of common law.

Other people around the world saw the abundance of America and assumed this was due to the system of liberty; they launched their own revolutions. The French were some of the first to revolt, and they did seem to achieve a certain abundance in the wake of this.

Poverty Declined

In gratitude, they donated the statue of Liberty Enlightening the World to America in 1886. This was their way of saying, thank you for teaching us that liberty is the source of prosperity. As the name implied, the upraised torch was the most important part of the statue.

Of course, we all know today that the torch is really quite meaningless. Prosperity actually has little to do with common law, the system of liberty, or any other such nonsense. It has to do with technological and industrial advancement wrought by enlightened government.

This advancement had lain dormant since the beginning of time, and it just happened to awaken, by coincidence, at the precise moment in history when liberty had awakened.

This was an amazing accident, and today thousands of scholars working in government-funded research projects, colleges, and universities have been unable to account for it.

Nevertheless, we all know it was an accident. Advancement comes not from common law or the system of liberty, but from dynamic, powerful government. In fact, the archaic common law has fallen into such disrepute that it is not even mentioned in schoolbooks.

This is a primary reason the Statue of Ellis Island had to be rebuilt and renamed. It was useless, a broken down structure dedicated to a broken down ideology.

In 1982, a publicity campaign was launched to solicit funds to rebuild not only the physical structure of the statue but also the statue's meaning.

The Lady's original meaning was absent from the deluge of pamphlets, news releases, and TV commercials. Nowhere was there even one line about common law. The System of Natural Liberty was not mentioned, nor were, of course, "effective economic calculation" or the free market.

Instead the Ellis Island Foundation accelerated a trend begun in 1903 when Emma Lazarus' poem, "Give me your tired, your poor, etc." was added to the statue. The Lady's connection with her original meaning was severed and she was forevermore linked with immigration.

One pamphlet, for instance, spoke of "the essential unity of the Statue of Liberty and Ellis Island." It first told the story of the immigrants, then explained that this story "reveals the meaning of the Statue of Liberty." A news release explained the statue had become "closely identified with the great flow of immigrants who landed on nearby Ellis Island. . . ."

. . . . The publicity campaign even swathed the statue in a mantle of nationalism, and tied its new meaning to the power of the government. The literature spoke of "the national symbol" and "the most powerful symbol." It praised "the grace and power" of this "national treasure," and of "the national monument."

Today as we move boldly forward into the 21st century, we have as our most important symbol, the Statue of Ellis Island. May we never forget its new meaning.

The Founding Fathers: Smugglers, Tax Evaders, and Traitors?[29]

By Richard J. Maybury

During patriotic holidays, the news media applaud the Founding Fathers. But rarely does anyone mention some important facts about them: that they were smugglers, tax evaders, and traitors.

Not only is this important, it is also praiseworthy; it produced the most advanced civilization ever known.

The Revolution is often said to have begun in 1775 at the Battle of Lexington. In truth, it began in the 16th century when the first colonists began traveling to the New World. Consider the hardships these people faced. Abandoning their relatives and friends, they boarded small leaky boats like the Mayflower—which was only as long as six automobiles—to spend months crossing 3,000 miles of storm-tossed ocean.

Many of these tiny, primitive vessels went down, yet as the years passed, more and more colonists risked their lives to make the journey. In THE OXFORD HISTORY OF THE AMERICAN PEOPLE, historian Samuel Eliot Morison tells us:

---

[29] Reprinted with permission from THE FREE MARKET, July 1987 issue, published by the Ludwig von Mises Institute, 518 West Magnolia Ave., Auburn, AL, 36832, ph: 800-636-4737, 334-321-2100, web site: www.mises.org

Gottlieb Mittelberger, who came to Philadelphia in 1750, described the misery during his voyage: bad drinking water and putrid salt meat, excessive heat and crowding, lice so thick that they could be scraped off the body, sea so rough that hatches were battened down and everyone vomited in the foul air; passengers succumbing to dysentery, scurvy, typhus, canker, and mouth-rot. Children under seven, he said, rarely survived the voyage, and in his ship no fewer than thirty-two died. One vessel carrying 400 Palatinate Germans from Rotterdam in August 1738 lost her master and three-quarters of the passengers before stranding on Block Island after a four-month journey.

Why? What in Europe could have been so horrible that rational people would risk their lives and their children's lives to escape it?

Socialism. It wasn't called socialism in those days, but that is what it was—unlimited government control and taxation of everything and everybody. There were no free markets and no free enterprise. Regardless of how honest or hard working a person was, it did him little good unless he was in bed with the government.

Out of desperation many rebelled. They evaded the controls and taxes, creating an underground economy. In ROOTS OF CAPITALISM, historian John Chamberlain writes that in France:

> For example, it took more than two thousand pages to print the rules established for the textile industry between 1666 and 1730. Weavers had to negotiate with the government for four years in order

to obtain permission to introduce "blackwarp" into their fabrics. The effect of the regulations was to freeze French textile production at a certain level, though smuggling and evasion of manufacturing regulations did alleviate the situation somewhat. The violation of the rules often brought terrible penalties: for breaking regulations governing printed calicoes some 16,000 people were either executed or killed in armed brushes with government agents.

America was a vast, uncharted wilderness beyond the reach of the politicians and tax collectors. It was nominally under the control of the European governments, but everyone knew it was too big and too far away for laws to be enforced there.

In short, America was a huge underground economy. Here trade was free and enterprise unrestricted. Taxes were so often evaded that for all practical purposes there were none; a person could keep everything he earned. He could save, and invest, and eventually have his own thriving business or farm that would provide jobs for the next wave of immigrants.

Inhabited by rebellious, individualistic smugglers and tax evaders, America quickly became the most prosperous place on earth.

You may have seen pictures of the Pine Tree Flag flown by American warships during the Revolution. Why would the colonists put a pine tree on their battle flag?

The (British) government had enacted a regulation saying no colonist could cut down tall, straight trees; these trees were to be reserved for masts on Navy ships. This meant the best, most valuable trees on a person's land had, in effect, been confiscated by the government.

When a government tree inspector would come through the forest to select and mark the best trees, colonists would follow him. These inspectors were highly trained experts, good at identifying the best trees for Navy ships—the Navy ships that were constantly pursuing smuggling ships.

When the government's lumberjacks then came through the forest to collect the marked trees, they would find the trees had already been cut and sold—for use on the smuggling ships.

One of these ships was THE LIBERTY, owned by John Hancock. Hancock was a successful wine merchant known throughout the colonies as "The Prince of Smugglers." His reputation eventually earned him the honor of being the first to sign the Declaration of Independence.

Unfortunately, as the story of the Pine Tree illustrates, America did not remain beyond the reach of government. As the colonists' wealth increased, politicians began making more and more efforts to steal—"tax"—this wealth. More and more bureaucrats and troops were sent to the colonies to enforce laws and shut down the underground economy.

The colonists' reaction was dramatic. The infamous Stamp Tax, for instance, was greeted by armed rebellion; tax collectors were tarred and feathered, a procedure which usually resulted in death. When John Hancock was arrested, the people rioted and the government's agents barely escaped with their lives.

This brings us to one of the most important but forgotten events in American history. In his 1818 analysis of the Revolution, John Adams spoke of it when he asked,

But what do we mean by the American Revolution? Do we mean the American War? The Revolution was effected before the war commenced. The Revolution was in the minds and hearts of the people, a change in their religious sentiments of their duties and obligations.

The key word here is religious. In Adams' analysis, he said a sermon delivered by Reverend Jonathan Mayhew on January 30, 1750, was "read by everybody" and was crucially important in leading to revolution.

In that sermon[30] Mayhew argued that there is a Higher Law than any government's law. The people, he said, are required to obey their government's law only when it is in agreement with Higher Law. Indeed, he argued, if the government violates Higher Law, "we are bound to throw off our allegiance" and "to resist."

What was this Higher Law?—the ancient common law which most colonists understood and obeyed faithfully even though they ridiculed and ignored the laws and taxes enacted by politicians.

Common law had evolved from two basic principles: 1) do all you have agreed to do, and 2) do not encroach on other persons or their property. These are the two principles on which all major religions and philosophies agree. Each expresses them a bit differently, but all agree on these two laws (and not much else).

These two laws are the source of all our essential prohibitions against theft, fraud, murder, rape, etc. "Do all you have

---

[30] To order a copy of Mayhew's Sermon and John Adams' remarks about it, contact Bluestocking Press, phone: 800-959-8586, web site: www.BluestockingPress.com

agreed to do" is the basis of contract law. "Do not encroach on other persons or their property" is the basis of criminal and tort law.

Common law was the law to which the American colonists were dedicated, and it was the law the politicians and bureaucrats were breaking—*they* were encroaching. So the colonists overthrew their government; they committed treason.

This is what the American Revolution was all about—treason. And, this treason was regarded as moral, ethical, and right in every way. It was derived straight from common law which was based on the people's religious beliefs. Wrote the great legal scholar Sir William Blackstone, "This law of nature, being coeval with mankind and dictated by God himself, is of course superior in obligation to any other...no human laws are of any validity if contrary to this."

Contrary to what we so often read, the Americans were not fighting the British. The Americans were British.

The war broke out at Lexington in April 1775, fifteen months before independence was declared. Therefore, for the first fifteen months of the war, America was still a part of Britain and Americans were still Englishmen fighting their own government. As many pamphlets and speeches explained, they were fighting for "The Rights of Englishmen!"

They were enforcing Higher Law. This eternal and immutable law said the politicians and bureaucrats were as human as anyone else and they had no special rights or privileges; they could not encroach on others. "All men are created equal," wrote Thomas Jefferson.

So, the most important and praiseworthy fact about the Founders which is rarely discussed is that they believed in a Higher Law than any government's law, and they did something about it. They evaded their government's taxes and regulations. They delivered speeches and wrote pamphlets informing others, and they eventually overthrew their government and set up a new one more closely in agreement with Higher Law.

The highly advanced, prosperous civilization we now enjoy was the direct result of their enforcement of Higher Law, and this civilization will continue only if Higher Law is re-applied, soon.

Recommended Authors

These authors are not statists. Generally their work is consistent with basic American principles. Many of these persons earn their livings primarily by writing about finance. This forces them to seek principles that reflect reality for, in their industry, a mistaken analysis can be immediately costly.

America's Founders
Adams, John
Adams, Samuel
Franklin, Benjamin
Hamilton, Alexander
Hancock, John
Henry, Patrick
Jay, John
Jefferson, Thomas
Madison, James
Mason, George
Paine, Thomas
Washington, George

**Children's Book Authors
ages 10 and up**
Greaves, Bettina B.
  (economics)
Heinlein, Robert
  (science fiction)
Hess, Karl (liberty & economics)
Lane, Rose Wilder
  (liberty & westward expansion)
Wilder, Laura Ingalls
  (liberty & westward expansion)

Economics
Bohm-Bawerk, Eugen von
Buchanan, James (nobel prize)
Fink, Richard
Friedman, David
Friedman, Milton
Greaves, Bettina B.
Greaves, Percy L.
Hayek, Friedrich A.
  (nobel prize)
Hazlitt, Henry
Maybury, Richard J.
Mises, Ludwig von
Rothbard, Murray N.
Sennholz, Hans F.
Skousen, Mark
Sowell, Thomas
Stigler, George Joseph
Webster, Pelatiah
Williams, Walter

Finance
Band, Richard E.
Bandow, Doug
Browne, Harry
Casey, Douglas
Davidson, James D.
Day, Adrian
North, Gary
Paul, Ron
Pugsley, John

History
Chamberlain, John
Weaver, Henry G.

Law
Bastiat, Frederic
Blackstone, William
Maybury, Richard J.
Spooner, Lysander

Philosophy
Hospers, John
Lane, Rose Wilder
Machan, Tibor R.
Thoreau, Henry David

Political
Bergland, David
Block, Walter
Childs, Roy A.
Chodorov, Frank
Harper, F.A.
Hess, Karl
Hummel, Jeffrey Rogers
Kirzner, Israel M.
Liggio, Leonard
MacBride, Roger
McElroy, Wendy
Mencken, H.L.
Poirot, Paul L.
Poole, Robert W. Jr.
Read, Leonard
Reed, Lawrence
Ringer, Robert J.
Samuels, Lawrence K.
Simon, William E.
Smith, George H.

Psychology
Branden, Nathaniel
Szasz, Thomas Stephen

Science Fiction, adult
Heinlein, Robert
Pournelle, Jerry
Smith, L. Neil

Organizations

- Advocates for Self-Government, 213 S. Erwin St., Cartersville, GA 30120, ph: 770-386-8372, 800-932-1776, web site: www.theadvocates.org

- Bluestocking Press, web site: www.BluestockingPress.com, ph: 800-959-8586 (For more information, see last page of this book.)

- Cato Institute, 1000 Massachusetts Ave NW, Washington, DC 20001, ph: 202-842-0200, web site: www.cato.org

- Contemporary Economics and Business Association (CEBA), PO Box 11471, Lynchburg, VA 24506, ph: 804-582-2338

- Foundation for Economic Education, 30 South Broadway, Irvington-on-Hudson, NY, 10533, ph: 800-960-4fee, 914-591-7230, web site: www.fee.org

- Foundation for Rational Economics and Education, PO Box 1776, Lake Jackson, TX 77566, ph: 979-265-3034, web site: www.nefl.org

- Institute for Humane Studies, George Mason University, 3301 N. Fairfax Dr., Ste. 440, Arlington, VA 22201, ph: 800-697-8799, 703-993-4880, web site: www.theihs.org

- Laissez Faire Books, 7123 Interstate 30, Ste. 42, Little Rock, AR 72209, ph: 800-326-0996, web site: LFB.com

- Liberty Tree, 100 Swan Way, Oakland, CA 94621, ph: 800-927-8733, 510-568-6047, web site: www.liberty-tree.org

- Pacific Research Institute, 755 Sansome St., Ste 450, San Francisco, CA 94111, ph: 415-989-0833, web site: www.pacificresearch.org

- Reason Foundation, 3415 S. Sepulveda Blvd., Ste. 400, Los Angeles, CA 90034, ph: 310-391-2245, web site: www.reason.com

About Richard J. Maybury

Richard Maybury, also known as Uncle Eric, is a world renowned author, lecturer, and geopolitical analyst. He consults with business firms in the U.S. and Europe. Richard is the former Global Affairs editor of MONEYWORLD and widely regarded as one of the finest free-market writers in America. Mr. Maybury's articles have appeared in THE WALL STREET JOURNAL, USA TODAY, and other major publications.

Richard Maybury has penned eleven books in the Uncle Eric series. His books have been endorsed by top business leaders including former U.S. Treasury Secretary William Simon, and he has been interviewed on more than 250 radio and TV shows across America.

He has been married for more than 35 years, has lived abroad, traveled around the world, and visited 48 states and 40 countries.

He is truly a teacher for all ages.

Index

P, Q

R

S

T

U, V

W, Y, Z

Published by Bluestocking Press

Uncle Eric Books by Richard J. Maybury

UNCLE ERIC TALKS ABOUT PERSONAL, CAREER, AND FINANCIAL SECURITY

WHATEVER HAPPENED TO PENNY CANDY?

WHATEVER HAPPENED TO JUSTICE?

ARE YOU LIBERAL? CONSERVATIVE? OR CONFUSED?

ANCIENT ROME: HOW IT AFFECTS YOU TODAY

EVALUATING BOOKS: WHAT WOULD THOMAS JEFFERSON THINK ABOUT THIS?

THE MONEY MYSTERY

THE CLIPPER SHIP STRATEGY

THE THOUSAND YEAR WAR IN THE MIDEAST

WORLD WAR I: THE REST OF THE STORY

WORLD WAR II: THE REST OF THE STORY

Bluestocking Guides (study guides for the Uncle Eric books)
by Jane A. Williams and/or Kathryn Daniels

Each Study Guide includes some or all of the following:
1) chapter-by-chapter comprehension questions and answers
2) application questions and answers
3) research activities
4) essay assignments
5) thought questions
6) final exam

More Bluestocking Press Titles

LAURA INGALLS WILDER AND ROSE WILDER LANE HISTORICAL TIMETABLE

CAPITALISM FOR KIDS: GROWING UP TO BE YOUR OWN BOSS by Karl Hess

COMMON SENSE BUSINESS FOR KIDS by Kathryn Daniels

ECONOMICS: A FREE MARKET READER edited by Jane Williams & Kathryn Daniels

Order information: Order any of the above by phone or online from:

Bluestocking Press

Phone: 800-959-8586

email: CustomerService@BluestockingPress.com

web site: www.BluestockingPress.com